READING
GALATIANS
with
JOHN STOTT

9 WEEKS FOR INDIVIDUALS OR GROUPS

JOHN STOTT
with DALE & SANDY LARSEN

An imprint of InterVarsity Press
Downers Grove, Illinois

InterVarsity Press
P.O. Box 1400, Downers Grove, IL 60515-1426
ivpress.com
email@ivpress.com

This volume is abridged and edited from The Message of Galatians *©1984 by John R. W. Stott, by permission of Inter-Varsity Press, England. Some of the discussion questions are from* Galatians: Experiencing the Grace of Christ *©1998 by John Stott with Dale and Sandy Larsen.*

InterVarsity Press® is the book-publishing division of InterVarsity Christian Fellowship/USA®, a movement of students and faculty active on campus at hundreds of universities, colleges, and schools of nursing in the United States of America, and a member movement of the International Fellowship of Evangelical Students. For information about local and regional activities, visit intervarsity.org.

All Scripture quotations, unless otherwise indicated, are taken from the Holy Bible, New International Version®, NIV®. Copyright © 1973, 1978, 1984, 2011 by Biblica, Inc.™ Used by permission of Zondervan. All rights reserved worldwide. www.zondervan.com The "NIV" and "New International Version" are trademarks registered in the United States Patent and Trademark Office by Biblica, Inc.™

Cover design: Cindy Kiple
Interior design: Beth McGill
Images: © f9photos / iStockphoto

ISBN 978-0-8308-3194-4 (print)
ISBN 978-0-8308-9240-2 (digital)

Library of Congress Cataloging-in-Publication Data

Names: Stott, John R. W., author.
Title: Reading Galatians with John Stott : 9 weeks for individuals or groups.
Description: Downers Grove : InterVarsity Press, 2017. | Series: Reading the Bible with John Stott (RBJS)
Identifiers: LCCN 2017013141 (print) | LCCN 2017016958 (ebook) | ISBN 9780830892402 (eBook) | ISBN 9780830831944 (pbk.)
Subjects: LCSH: Bible. Galatians—Textbooks.
Classification: LCC BS2685.55 (ebook) | LCC BS2685.55 .S764 2017 (print) | DDC 227/.40071—dc23
LC record available at https://lccn.loc.gov/2017013141

P	20	19	18	17	16	15	14	13	12	11	10	9	8	7	6	5	4	3	2	1
Y	33	32	31	30	29	28	27	26	25	24	23	22	21	20	19	18	17			

Contents

How to Read the Bible
with John Stott

❦

During John Stott's life (1921–2011), he was one of the world's master Bible teachers. Christians on every continent heard and read John Stott's exposition of Scripture, which was at once instructive and inspiring. With over eight million copies of his more than fifty books sold in dozens of languages, it is not surprising that *Time* magazine recognized him in 2005 as one of the "100 Most Influential People in the World" and *Christianity Today* called him "evangelicalism's premier teacher and preacher." At the core of his ministry were the Bible and his beloved Bible Speaks Today series, which he originated as New Testament series editor. He himself contributed several volumes to the series, which have now been edited for this Reading the Bible with John Stott series.

The purpose of this series is to offer excerpts of Stott's *The Message of Galatians* in brief readings, suitable for daily use. Though Stott was himself an able scholar, this series avoids technicalities and scholarly debates, with each reading emphasizing the substance, significance, and application of the text.

Following each set of six readings is found a discussion guide. This can be used by individuals to help them dig more deeply into the text. It can also be used by study groups meeting regularly. Individuals in the groups can go through the readings between group meetings and then use the discussion guide to help the group understand and apply the Scripture passage. Discussions are designed to last between forty-five and sixty minutes. Guidelines for leaders at the end of this volume offer many helpful suggestions for having a successful meeting.

If you are a group member, you can help everyone present in the following ways:

1. Read and pray through the readings before you meet.

2. Be willing to participate in the discussion. The leader won't be lecturing. Instead all will be asked to discuss what they have learned.

3. Stick to the topic being discussed. The focus is the particular passage of Scripture. Only rarely should you refer to other portions of the Bible or outside sources. This will allow everyone to participate on equal footing.

4. Listen attentively to what others have to say. Be careful not to talk too much but encourage a balanced discussion among all participants. You may be surprised by what you can learn from others. Generally, questions do not have one right answer but are intended to encourage various dimensions of the text.

5. Expect God to teach you through the passage and through what others have to say.

6. Use the following guidelines and read them at the start of the first session.

- We will make the group a safe place by keeping confidential what is said in the group about personal matters.

- We will provide time for each person to talk who wants to.

- We will listen attentively to each other.

- We will talk about ourselves and our own situations, avoiding conversation about others.

- We will be cautious about giving advice to one another.

John Stott had an immense impact on the church in the last half of the twentieth century. With these volumes readers today can continue to benefit from the riches of the Bible that Stott opened to millions.

Introduction

In the course of the thirty years or so between his conversion outside Damascus and his imprisonment in Rome, the apostle Paul traveled widely through the empire as an ambassador of Jesus Christ. On his three famous missionary journeys, he preached the gospel and planted churches in the provinces of Galatia, Asia, Macedonia (northern Greece), and Achaia (southern Greece). His visits were followed by his letters, by which he helped to supervise the churches he had founded.

One of these letters, believed to be his earliest (AD 48 or 49), is the letter to the Galatians. It is addressed "To the churches in Galatia." There is some dispute as to what is meant by Galatia. I take the view that it refers to the southern part of the province, in particular to the four cities of Pisidian Antioch, Iconium, Lystra, and Derbe, which Paul evangelized during his first missionary journey (see Acts 13–14). In each of these four cities there was now a church.

In the New Testament, what is called "the church of God" (Galatians 1:13), the universal church, is divided into local churches, which are not denominations but congregations. These churches were grouped together because of geographical and political considerations. Such a group of churches could be described either in the plural or by a singular collective noun. This usage implies some biblical warrant for the concept of a regional church, the federation of local churches in a particular area.

Already in the first paragraph of his letter, Paul touches on two themes he will constantly return to: his apostleship and his gospel. In the ancient world all letters began with the writer's name, followed by the recipient's name and a greeting or message. But in his letter to the Galatians, Paul enlarges more than was customary in those days, and more than he does in his other letters, both on his credentials as a writer and on his message. He has good reasons for doing so.

Since his visit to these Galatian cities, the churches he founded have been troubled by false teachers. These people have mounted a powerful attack on Paul's authority and gospel. They contradict his gospel of justification by grace alone through faith alone, insisting that more than faith in Christ is needed for salvation. You have to be circumcised as well, they say, and keep all the law of Moses (see Acts 15:1, 5). Having undermined Paul's gospel, they proceed to undermine his authority also. "Who is this fellow Paul, anyway?" they ask scornfully. "He certainly wasn't one of the twelve apostles of Jesus. Nor, so far as we know, has he received any authorization from anybody. He is just a self-appointed impostor."

Paul sees the dangers of this two-pronged attack; so right at the beginning of the letter he plunges into a statement of his apostolic authority and of his gospel of grace. He will elaborate these themes later in the letter, but notice how he begins: "Paul, an apostle [not an impostor]. . . . Grace and peace to you." The two terms *apostle* and *grace* were loaded words in that situation; and if we understand their meaning, we have grasped the two main subjects of the letter to the Galatians.

John Stott

1

Galatians 1:1-12

False Teachers and Faithless Christians

❦

Paul, an Apostle

GALATIANS 1:1-2

> ¹Paul, an apostle—sent not from men nor by a man, but by Jesus Christ and God the Father, who raised him from the dead—²and all the brothers and sisters with me,
>
> To the churches in Galatia:

Paul claims for himself the very title that the false teachers were evidently denying him. He was an apostle of Jesus Christ. This is the title Jesus used for his special representatives or delegates. From the wider company of disciples he chose twelve, named them "apostles," and sent them out to preach. Thus they were personally chosen, called, and commissioned by Jesus Christ and authorized to teach in his name. The word *apostle* was not a general word that could be applied to every Christian like the words *believer*, *saint*, *brother*, or *sister*. It was a special term reserved for the Twelve and for one or two others the risen Christ had personally appointed.

Paul claimed to belong to this select company of apostles. Notice how he clearly distinguishes himself from other Christians who were with him at the time of writing. He calls them "all the brothers and sisters with me." He is happy to associate them with him in the salutation, but he unashamedly puts himself first and gives himself a title that he does not give to them. He alone among them is an apostle.

Paul leaves us in no doubt about the nature of his apostleship. He makes a forceful statement that his apostolic commission was neither directly nor indirectly human; it was wholly divine. It was "by Jesus Christ and God the Father, who raised him from the dead." God the Father chose Paul to be an apostle and appointed him to this office through Jesus Christ, whom he raised from the dead. It was the risen Lord who commissioned Paul on the Damascus road, and in his letters Paul several times refers to this sight of the risen Christ as an essential condition of his apostleship.

Why did Paul assert and defend his apostleship? It was because the gospel that he preached was at stake. If Paul were not an apostle of Jesus Christ, then people could, and no doubt would, reject his gospel. This he could not bear. For what Paul spoke was Christ's message on Christ's authority. So he defended his apostolic authority in order to defend his message.

A Rescue Religion

GALATIANS 1:3-5

> [3]Grace and peace to you from God our Father and the Lord Jesus Christ, [4]who gave himself for our sins to rescue us from the present evil age, according to the will of our God and Father, [5]to whom be glory for ever and ever. Amen.

As in all his letters, Paul sends the Galatians a message of grace and peace. These are no formal and meaningless terms. They are filled with theological substance. In fact, they summarize Paul's gospel of salvation. The nature of salvation is peace, or reconciliation—peace with God, peace with others, peace within. The source of salvation is grace, God's free favor, regardless of any human merit or works, his lovingkindness to the undeserving. And this grace and peace flow from the Father and the Son together.

Paul immediately goes on to the great historical event in which God's grace was exhibited and from which his peace is derived, namely, the death of Jesus Christ on the cross. Although Paul has declared that God the Father raised Christ from the dead, he writes now that it was by giving himself to die on the cross that he saves us.

The character of Christ's death is indicated in the expression "who gave himself for our sins." The death of Jesus Christ was primarily neither a display of love nor an example of heroism, but a sacrifice for sin. Christ's death was a sin offering, the unique sacrifice by which our sins may be forgiven and put away. He bore in his righteous person the curse or judgment that our sins deserved.

If the nature of Christ's death on the cross was "for our sins," its object was "to rescue us from the present evil age." Christianity is a rescue religion. From what does Christ rescue us by his death? Not from the evil world but from this evil *age*. Christian conversion means being rescued from the old age and being transferred into the new age, "the age to come." The Christian life means living in this age the life of the age to come. The purpose of Christ's death, therefore, was not only to bring us forgiveness, but that, having been forgiven, we should live a new life, the life of the age to come.

Both our rescue out of this present evil age and the means by which it has been effected are "according to the will of our God and Father." We must never imply either that the Son volunteered to do something against the Father's will or that the Father required the Son to do something against his own will. In the cross the will of the Father and the will of the Son were in perfect harmony.

No wonder Paul ends this first section of his letter with a doxology: "to whom be glory [the glory that is his due, the glory that belongs to him] for ever and ever. Amen."

A Different Gospel?

GALATIANS 1:6

> [6]I am astonished that you are so quickly deserting the one who called you to live in the grace of Christ and are turning to a different gospel—

In every other letter, after greeting his readers, Paul goes on to pray for them or to praise and thank God. Only in the letter to the

Galatians are there no prayer, no praise, no thanksgiving, and no commendation. Instead he addresses himself to his theme at once with a note of extreme urgency. He expresses astonishment at the fickleness and instability of the Galatians.

The Galatians are religious turncoats, spiritual deserters. They are turning away from him who called them in the grace of Christ and are embracing another gospel. The true gospel is good news of a God who is gracious to undeserving sinners. But the Galatian converts, who had received this gospel of grace, were now turning away to another gospel, a gospel of works.

The false teachers who were influencing them were evidently "Judaizers." They did not deny that you must believe in Jesus for salvation, but they stressed that you must be circumcised and keep the law as well. In other words, by your obedience to the law you must finish what Christ has begun. You must add your works to the work of Christ.

This doctrine Paul simply will not tolerate. Add human merits to the merit of Christ and human works to the work of Christ? God forbid! The work of Christ is a finished work; the gospel of Christ is a gospel of free grace. Salvation is by grace alone, through faith alone, without any admixture of human works or merits. It is due solely to God's gracious call and not to any good works of our own.

Paul goes further than this. He says that the defection of the Galatian converts was in their experience as well as in their theology. He accuses them not of deserting the gospel of grace for another gospel, but of "deserting *the one* who called" them in grace. Theology and experience, Christian faith and

Christian life, belong together and cannot be separated. Let the Galatians beware, who have so readily and rashly started turning away. It is impossible to forsake the gospel without forsaking God. To turn from the gospel of grace is to turn from the God of grace.

False Teaching Causes Turmoil

GALATIANS 1:7

> [7]which is really no gospel at all. Evidently some people are throwing you into confusion and are trying to pervert the gospel of Christ.

False teachers had thrown the Galatian congregations into a state of turmoil—intellectual confusion on the one hand and warring factions on the other. It is interesting that the Council at Jerusalem, which probably met just after Paul wrote this letter, would use the same verb in their letter to the churches: "We have heard that some went out from us without our authorization and *disturbed* you, troubling your minds by what they said" (Acts 15:24).

This trouble was caused by false doctrine. The Judaizers were trying to "pervert" the gospel of Christ. They were not just corrupting the gospel but reversing it, turning it back to front and upside down. You cannot modify or supplement the gospel without radically changing its character.

So the two chief characteristics of the false teachers are that they were troubling the church and changing the gospel. These two go together. To tamper with the gospel is always to trouble the church. You cannot touch the gospel and leave the church untouched, because the church is created and lives by the gospel.

Indeed, the church's greatest troublemakers (now as then) are not those outside who oppose, ridicule, and persecute it, but those inside who try to change the gospel. They are the ones who trouble the church. Conversely, the only way to be a good church person is to be a good gospel person. The best way to serve the church is to believe and to preach the gospel.

Under God's Curse

GALATIANS 1:8-9

> [8]But even if we or an angel from heaven should preach a gospel other than the one we preached to you, let them be under God's curse! [9]As we have already said, so now I say again: If anybody is preaching to you a gospel other than what you accepted, let them be under God's curse!

After utter astonishment, Paul's second reaction to the situation in Galatia was indignation over the false teachers. Now he pronounces a solemn curse on them. The Greek word translated "under God's curse" is *anathema*. It was used in the Greek Old Testament for the divine ban, the curse of God that rested upon anything or anyone devoted by him to destruction. So the apostle Paul desires that these false teachers should come under the divine ban, curse, or *anathema*. That is, he expresses the wish that God's judgment will fall upon them.

Should we dismiss this *anathema* as an intemperate outburst? Should we reject it as a sentiment inconsistent with the Spirit of Christ and unworthy of the gospel of Christ? At least two considerations indicate that this apostolic *anathema* was not the expression of Paul's personal venom toward rival teachers.

The first consideration is that the curse of the apostle, or the curse of God that the apostle desires, is universal in its scope. It rests upon any and every teacher who distorts the essence of the gospel and propagates this distortion. Paul even desires the curse of God to fall upon *himself*, should he be guilty of perverting it. The second consideration is that his curse is uttered deliberately and with conscious responsibility to God. Paul utters his *anathema* both impartially (whoever the teachers might be) and deliberately (in the presence of Christ his Lord).

Why did Paul feel so strongly and use such drastic language? Two reasons are plain. The first is that the glory of Christ was at stake. To make human works necessary to salvation, even as a supplement to the work of Christ, is derogatory to his finished work. It implies that Christ's work was in some way unsatisfactory and that people need to add to it and improve on it. The second reason is that the good of people's souls was also at stake. Paul was not writing about some trivial doctrine but about something fundamental to the gospel. Nor was he speaking of those who merely *hold* false views, but of those who *teach* them and mislead others by their teaching.

To many it is inconceivable that we should desire false teachers to fall under the curse of God and be treated as such by the church. But if we cared more for the glory of Christ and for the good of people's souls, we too would not be able to bear the corruption of the gospel of grace.

Substance and Source

GALATIANS 1:10-12

> [10]Am I now trying to win the approval of human beings, or of God? Or am I trying to please people? If I were still trying to please people, I would not be a servant of Christ.
>
> [11]I want you to know, brothers and sisters, that the gospel I preached is not of human origin. [12]I did not receive it from any man, nor was I taught it; rather, I received it by revelation from Jesus Christ.

It seems that Paul's detractors accused him of being a people pleaser who suited his message to his audience. But since Paul is first and foremost a servant of Jesus Christ, his ambition is to please Christ, not people. It is therefore as "a servant of Christ," responsible to his divine Lord, that he has measured his words and has dared to utter his solemn *anathema*.

Paul insists that there is only one gospel and that this gospel does not change. There are certainly different gospels being preached, but that is what they are—*different*. The message of the false teachers was not an alternative gospel; it was a perverted gospel.

How can we recognize the true gospel? Paul gives us its marks. They concern its substance (what it is) and its source (where it comes from).

The true gospel is the gospel of grace, of God's free and unmerited favor. Whenever teachers start exalting humankind, implying that we can contribute anything to our salvation by our own morality, religion, philosophy, or respectability, the gospel of grace is being corrupted. The true gospel magnifies the free grace of God.

The second test concerns the gospel's origin. The true gospel is the gospel of the apostles of Jesus Christ—the New Testament gospel. The criterion by which we test all systems and opinions is the primitive gospel, the gospel that the apostles preached and is now recorded in the New Testament.

But where did Paul get this wonderful gospel? Was it the product of his own fertile brain? Did he make it up? Or was it stale secondhand stuff with no original authority? Did he crib it from the other apostles in Jerusalem, which the Judaizers evidently maintained?

Paul's answer to these questions is found in verses 11 and 12. "I preached this gospel," Paul could say, "but I did not invent it. Nor did I receive it from others, as if it were already an accepted tradition handed down from a previous generation. Nor was I taught it, so that I had to learn it from human teachers." Instead, "it came through a revelation of Jesus Christ."

As in verse 1 Paul asserted the divine origin of his apostolic commission, so now he asserts the divine origin of his apostolic gospel. Neither his mission nor his message was derived from human beings; both came to him direct from God and Jesus Christ. He is affirming that his message is not his message but God's message, that his gospel is not his gospel but God's gospel, that his words are not his words but God's words.

Galatians 1:1-12

....

DISCUSSION GUIDE

OPEN

How do you test the truth of what you hear from public figures, your pastor, and other Christian teachers?

STUDY

Read Galatians 1:1-12.

1. What key themes emerge in verses 1-5 in response to the controversy with the false teachers?

2. In light of the controversy, how was it significant for Paul to say he is an apostle "sent not from men nor by a man, but by Jesus Christ and God the Father"?

3. Create an outline of the gospel based on verses 1-5.

4. In his other letters, after greeting his readers, Paul goes on to pray for them or to praise and thank God. In contrast, what does he do in this letter?

5. The Greek word in verse 6 for "deserting" means "to transfer one's allegiance." It is used for soldiers in the army

who revolt or desert, and those who change sides in politics or philosophy. How is it appropriate for the Galatians as they are described here?

6. The false teachers were trying to "pervert" the gospel (v. 7) or, according to the Greek, to completely "reverse" the meaning of the gospel. Thus the Galatians were forsaking the gospel of grace for a gospel of works. Create a chart contrasting these two ways of thinking—grace and works—as you understand them.

7. How do you account for Paul's strong words against the teachers in verses 8-9?

8. Verses 8-9 tell us that we are to judge the teacher by the gospel and not judge the gospel by the teacher. Why is this distinction important?

9. Why does Paul add the disclaimer of verse 10?

10. The popular view is that there are many ways to God and that the gospel changes with the changing years. How could you argue against that using Paul's perspective in this Scripture passage?

APPLY

1. Who do you know who is being swayed by false teaching, and how can you help that person?

2. When are you likely to judge the gospel according to a teacher rather than judging the teacher by the gospel?

Galatians 1:13–2:10
Radical Change

❧

God Changes a Fanatic

GALATIANS 1:13-16

¹³For you have heard of my previous way of life in Judaism, how intensely I persecuted the church of God and tried to destroy it. ¹⁴I was advancing in Judaism beyond many of my own age among my people and was extremely zealous for the traditions of my fathers. ¹⁵But when God, who set me apart from my mother's womb and called me by his grace, was pleased ¹⁶to reveal his Son in me so that I might preach him among the Gentiles, my immediate response was not to consult any human being.

Having made his startling claim to a direct revelation from God without human means, Paul goes on to prove it from history, that is, from the facts of his own autobiography. The situation before his conversion, at his conversion, and after his conversion were such that he clearly got his gospel not from any human being but directly from God.

The apostle describes his preconversion state *in Judaism*, while he was still practicing the Jewish religion. What he was like in those days was well known. He mentions two aspects of his unregenerate days: his persecution of the church, which he now knows to be "the church of God," and his enthusiasm for Jewish religious traditions. In both, he says, he was fanatical.

Take his persecution of the church. Paul persecuted the church of God "intensely." The phrase indicates the violence, even the savagery, with which he set about this grim work. Not satisfied with *persecuting* the church, he was actually bent on *destroying* it.

He was equally fanatical in his enthusiasm for Jewish traditions. "I was advancing in Judaism beyond many of my own age among my people and was extremely zealous for the traditions of my fathers." He had been brought up according to the strictest party of the Jewish religion, namely, as a Pharisee, and that is how he had lived.

So before his conversion Saul of Tarsus was a bigot and a fanatic, wholehearted in his devotion to Judaism and in his persecution of Christ and the church. Now a man in that mental and emotional state is in no mood to change his mind or even to have it changed for him by others. No conditioned reflex or other psychological device could convert a man in that state. Only God could reach him—and God did!

The contrast between verses 13 and 14 on the one hand and verses 15 and 16 on the other is dramatically abrupt. In verses 13 and 14 Paul speaks about himself: "*I* persecuted the church of God, *I* tried to destroy it, *I* advanced in Judaism, *I* was extremely zealous." But in verses 15 and 16 he begins to speak of God. It was *God* who "set me apart from my mother's womb," *God* who "called me by his grace" and *God* who "was pleased to reveal his Son in me." In other words, "in my fanaticism I was bent upon a course of persecution and destruction, but God (who I had left out of my calculations) arrested me and changed my headlong course. All my raging fanaticism was no match for the good pleasure of God."

An Independent Gospel

GALATIANS 1:17-24

> [17]I did not go up to Jerusalem to see those who were apostles before I was, but I went into Arabia. Later I returned to Damascus.
>
> [18]Then after three years, I went up to Jerusalem to get acquainted with Cephas and stayed with him fifteen days. [19]I saw none of the other apostles—only James, the Lord's brother. [20]I assure you before God that what I am writing you is no lie.
>
> [21]Then I went to Syria and Cilicia. [22]I was personally unknown to the churches of Judea that are in Christ. [23]They only heard the report: "The man who formerly persecuted us is now preaching the faith he once tried to destroy." [24]And they praised God because of me.

Paul produces a series of three "alibis" to prove that he did not spend time in Jerusalem having his gospel shaped by the other apostles.

Alibi 1. He went into Arabia (v. 17). According to Acts 9:20, Paul spent a little while in Damascus preaching, which suggests that his gospel was sufficiently clearly defined for him to announce it. But it must have been soon afterward that he went into Arabia, likely for quiet and solitude. He seems to have stayed there for three years. During this period of withdrawal, as he meditated on the Old Testament Scriptures, on what he already knew about Jesus, and on his experience of conversion, the gospel of the grace of God was revealed to him in its fullness.

Alibi 2. He went up to Jerusalem later and briefly (vv. 18-20). Paul is quite open about this visit to Jerusalem, but he makes light of it. It was not nearly as significant as the false teachers were obviously suggesting. For one thing, it took place after three years, which almost certainly means three years after his conversion. By that time his gospel would have been fully formulated. Next, when he reached Jerusalem, he saw only two of the apostles, Peter and James. Third, he was in Jerusalem for only fifteen days. Of course in fifteen days the apostles would have had some time to talk about Christ. But Paul's point is that he had no time to absorb from Peter the whole counsel of God. Besides, that was not the purpose of his visit. Much of those two weeks in Jerusalem, we learn from Acts 9:28-29, was spent in preaching.

Alibi 3. He went off to Syria and Cilicia (vv. 21-24). This visit to the extreme north corresponds to Acts 9:30, where we are told that Paul, who was already in danger for his life, was brought by the believers to Caesarea and then sent off to Tarsus, which is in Cilicia. Since he says here that he went to Syria as well, he may have revisited Damascus and called at Antioch on his way to

Tarsus. The point Paul is making is that he was up in the far north, nowhere near Jerusalem.

As we will see in Galatians 2:1, not until fourteen years after his conversion did Paul revisit Jerusalem and have a more prolonged consultation with the other apostles. By that time his gospel was fully developed. During the fourteen-year period between his conversion and this consultation, he had paid only one brief and insignificant visit to Jerusalem. The rest of the time he had spent in distant Arabia, Syria, and Cilicia. His alibis proved the independence of his gospel.

A Critical Consultation

GALATIANS 2:1-2

> ¹Then after fourteen years, I went up again to Jerusalem, this time with Barnabas. I took Titus along also. ²I went in response to a revelation and, meeting privately with those esteemed as leaders, I presented to them the gospel that I preach among the Gentiles. I wanted to be sure I was not running and had not been running my race in vain.

Wherever Paul went, the false teachers dogged his footsteps. No sooner had he planted the gospel in some locality than false teachers began to trouble the church by perverting it. Further, in order to discredit Paul's message, they also challenged his authority.

Paul's detractors have plenty of successors in the Christian church today. They tell us that we do not need to pay too much attention to his writings. They forget or deny that he was an apostle of Jesus Christ, uniquely called, commissioned, authorized, and inspired to teach in his name.

One way the false teachers of Paul's day tried to undermine his authority was to hint that his gospel was different from Peter's gospel and indeed from the views of all the other apostles in Jerusalem. They were trying to disrupt the unity of the apostolic circle.

Paul has already shown that his gospel came from God, not from human teachers. He now shows that his gospel is precisely the same as that of the other apostles. To prove that his gospel is identical with theirs, he stresses that when he paid a proper visit to Jerusalem, his gospel was endorsed and approved by them. There are two important aspects of this visit, namely, his companions and his message.

His companions were Barnabas and Titus. What is particularly remarkable is that Barnabas was a Jew, while Titus was a Greek. That is, Titus was an uncircumcised Gentile, himself a product of the very Gentile mission that was in dispute and the Judaizers were challenging.

His message, the gospel he preached to the Gentiles, he now laid before the other apostles. He says he did it "to be sure I was not running and had not been running my race in vain." He had no personal doubts or misgivings about his gospel and did not need the reassurance of the other Jerusalem apostles, for he had been preaching it for fourteen years, but rather he did not want his ministry, past and present, to be rendered fruitless by the Judaizers. It was to overthrow their influence, not to strengthen his own conviction, that he laid his gospel before the Jerusalem apostles.

It was a tense and crucial situation, an occasion fraught with great peril and equally great possibility for the subsequent history of the Christian church. What would be the reaction of the apostles in Jerusalem to Paul's Gentile companion and Gentile mission? Would the liberty with which Christ has made us free be maintained, or would the church be condemned to bondage and sterility?

A Victory for Freedom

GALATIANS 2:3-5

> [3]Yet not even Titus, who was with me, was compelled to be circumcised, even though he was a Greek. [4]This matter arose because some false believers had infiltrated our ranks to spy on the freedom we have in Christ Jesus and to make us slaves. [5]We did not give in to them for a moment, so that the truth of the gospel might be preserved for you.

It was a daring step for Paul to take Titus with him to Jerusalem. To introduce a Gentile into the headquarters of the Jerusalem church could be interpreted as a deliberate act of provocation. In a sense, it probably was, although Paul's motive was not provocative. It was not in order to stir up strife that he brought Titus with him, but in order to establish the truth of the gospel. This truth is that Jews and Gentiles are accepted by God on the same terms, namely, through faith in Jesus Christ, and must therefore be accepted by the church without any discrimination between them.

The point was made and the truth established: "Not even Titus, who was with me, was compelled to be circumcised, even though he was a Greek." However, the victory was not won without a battle, for strong pressure was exerted on Paul to circumcise Titus. This came from "false believers," almost certainly Judaizers, and Paul has stern words to say about them. They had "infiltrated our ranks." This may mean either that they had no business to be in the church fellowship at all, or that they had gate crashed the private conference with the apostles. In either case, in Paul's view they were spies. In particular, they tried to insist on Titus being circumcised. We know that this was the platform of the Judaizing party, for their slogan is given us in Acts 15:1: "Unless you are circumcised, according to the custom taught by Moses, you cannot be saved."

Paul saw the issue plainly. It was not just a question of circumcision and uncircumcision, of Gentile and Jewish customs. It was a matter of fundamental importance regarding the truth of the gospel, namely, of Christian freedom versus bondage. The Christian has been set free from the law in the sense that our acceptance before God depends entirely on God's grace in the death of Jesus Christ received by faith. To introduce the works of the law and make our acceptance depend on our obedience to rules and regulations was to bring a free person into bondage again. Titus was a test case of this principle. He was an uncircumcised Gentile, but he was a converted Christian. Having believed in Jesus, he had been accepted by God in Christ, and that, Paul said, was enough.

Paul's Gospel Affirmed

GALATIANS 2:6-9a

> ⁶As for those who were held in high esteem—whatever they were makes no difference to me; God does not show

favoritism—they added nothing to my message. ⁷On the contrary, they recognized that I had been entrusted with the task of preaching the gospel to the uncircumcised, just as Peter had been to the circumcised. ⁸For God, who was at work in Peter as an apostle to the circumcised, was also at work in me as an apostle to the Gentiles. ⁹James, Cephas and John, those esteemed as pillars, gave me and Barnabas the right hand of fellowship when they recognized the grace given to me.

As we have already seen, Paul had a private interview with the Jerusalem apostles. They are identified here by name: James the Lord's brother, Peter, and John.

In other places in this paragraph, however, Paul uses indirect expressions to describe these apostles. They are "those esteemed as leaders" (v. 2), "those who were held in high esteem" (v. 6), and "those esteemed as pillars" (v. 9). In each case Paul alludes to them according to their repute. He is not being derogatory to them, for he has acknowledged them already in Galatians 1:17 as "those who were apostles before I was," and he tells us here that they gave him "the right hand of fellowship."

Why then does he refer to them in this roundabout way? Probably his expressions were influenced by the fact that the Judaizers exaggerated the status of the Jerusalem apostles at the expense of his own. Perhaps the false believers were drawing attention to what they regarded as the superior qualifications of James, Peter, and John—that James was one of the Lord's brothers, and that Peter and John had belonged to the inner circle of three. Besides, they had known Jesus in the days of his flesh, which Paul probably had not. Paul means no disrespect or denial of their apostolic authority. He simply indicates that, although he accepts their *office* as apostles, he is not overawed by their *person* as it was being inflated by the Judaizers.

Paul mentions two results of his consultation with the Jerusalem apostles.

First, "they added nothing to my message." In other words, they did not find Paul's gospel defective or lacking anything. It is as if Paul wrote to the Galatians, "The gospel that I am preaching today was not altered by the Jerusalem apostles. It is the same as I preached before I saw them. It is the gospel I preached to you and you received. I have added nothing, subtracted nothing, changed nothing. It is you Galatians, not I, who are deserting the gospel."

Second, they "gave me and Barnabas the right hand of fellowship." They recognized that they and Paul had been entrusted with the same gospel. The only difference between them was that they had been allocated different spheres in which to preach it. Operating in different areas of influence, they would still enjoy their common fellowship in Christ.

Apostles in Agreement

GALATIANS 2:9b-10

> [9b]They agreed that we should go to the Gentiles, and they to the circumcised. [10]All they asked was that we should continue to remember the poor, the very thing I had been eager to do all along.

From the references to the Gentiles and the "circumcised" (Jews) in verses 8-9, we should not imagine that there are two gospels, one for Gentiles and one for Jews. There is one gospel, but different apostles were called to bring it into different spheres of influence. The Jerusalem apostles agreed that Paul and his associates should evangelize chiefly in Gentile areas, while they evangelized chiefly to their fellow Jews.

They also added that they wanted Paul and Barnabas to "remember the poor," the poverty-stricken churches of Judea, which Paul was already "eager to do." As we saw earlier, it was primarily for famine relief that he and Barnabas were in Jerusalem at that time. And he continued to care for the poor in the following years. He urged the more wealthy Gentile churches of Macedonia and Achaia to support the poorer churches of Judea, and regarded their gift as a means to foster and demonstrate Jewish-Gentile solidarity in the fellowship of the Christian church.

Looking back over the first paragraph of Galatians 2, we have learned that on his second visit to Jerusalem Paul met two groups whose attitude toward him differed completely. The false believers, who disagreed with his gospel and his policy, tried to compel Titus to be circumcised. Paul refused to submit to them. The apostles, on the other hand, acknowledged the truth of Paul's gospel and gave him their hand in confirmation.

In the New Testament the apostles of Jesus Christ do not contradict one another. Certainly there are differences of *style* between them, because their inspiration did not obliterate their individual personalities. There are also differences of *emphasis*, because they were called to different spheres and preached or wrote to different audiences. They had different commissions, but they had a common message.

If there is only one gospel in the New Testament, there is only one gospel for the church. Whether it is preached to young or old, to east or west, to Jews or Gentiles, to cultured or uncultured, to scientists or nonscientists, although its presentation may vary, its substance is the same: the apostolic faith, a recognizable body of doctrine taught by the apostles of Jesus Christ and preserved for us in the New Testament.

Galatians 1:13–2:10

Discussion Guide

Open

When someone you know undergoes a radical change, what questions does it raise for you?

Study

Read Galatians 1:13–2:10.

1. What were the driving forces in Paul's life before his conversion?

2. How does Paul's preconversion life add weight to his claim that his gospel came from God?

3. What steps did Paul take to deliberately avoid human consultation about the gospel?

4. At the beginning of his Christian life, Paul did not totally avoid other Christians, but he restricted his contacts. What did his caution accomplish in his life?

5. Given his reputation, how might Paul have expected the churches to respond to him as a supposed new believer?

6. What significance do you see in the fact that the Christians in Judea "praised God because of" Paul, rather than praising Paul?

7. Why was it wise for Paul to keep his meeting with the apostles private?

8. What is significant about the apostles' response to Titus?

9. Paul implies that giving in to the false teachers would mean a descent into slavery. In what senses could a Christian become a slave?

10. What did the apostles in Jerusalem have to be convinced of in order to accept Paul's preaching?

11. What significance do you find in the fact that the apostles accepted Paul's ministry when they saw the grace given to him (v. 9) rather than the persuasive gifts or intelligence or preaching abilities given to him?

12. What are some distorted versions of the gospel you have heard, and how did you discover that these versions had altered the true gospel?

APPLY

1. Think of some Christian groups whose style grates on your nerves. How does seeing that there is only one gospel help your acceptance of them?

2. Think of some Christian groups who choose to emphasize things you don't think are crucial. How does seeing that there is only one gospel affect your understanding of them?

3

Galatians 2:11-21
Facing Conflict

❦

A Dramatic Encounter

> [11]When Cephas came to Antioch, I opposed him to his face, because he stood condemned. [12]For before certain men came from James, he used to eat with the Gentiles. But when they arrived, he began to draw back and separate himself from the Gentiles because he was afraid of those who belonged to the circumcision group. [13]The other Jews joined him in his hypocrisy, so that by their hypocrisy even Barnabas was led astray.

This is one of the most tense and dramatic episodes in the New Testament. Here are two leading apostles of Jesus Christ face to face in complete and open conflict.

Both Paul and Peter were Christian men, men of God, who knew what it is to be forgiven through Christ and to receive the

Holy Spirit. Further, they were both apostles of Jesus Christ, specially called, commissioned, and invested with authority by him. They were both honored in the churches for their leadership. They had both been mightily used by God. In fact, the book of Acts is virtually divided in half by them, the first part telling the story of Peter and the second part telling the story of Paul.

Yet here is the apostle Paul opposing the apostle Peter to his face, contradicting him, rebuking him, condemning him, because Peter had withdrawn and separated himself from Gentile Christian believers and would no longer eat with them. It was not that Peter denied the gospel in his *teaching*, for Paul has been at pains to show that he and the Jerusalem apostles were at one in their understanding of the gospel. Peter's offense against the gospel was in his *conduct*.

When Peter first arrived in Antioch, he ate with Gentile Christians. His old Jewish scruples had been overcome. He did not consider himself in any way defiled or contaminated by contact with uncircumcised Gentile Christians, as once he would have thought.

Then one day a group arrived in Antioch from Jerusalem, posing as apostolic delegates. These Judaizing teachers won a notable convert in the person of the apostle Peter. For Peter, who had previously eaten with these Gentile Christians, now withdrew from them and separated himself. He seems to have taken this action shamefacedly.

Paul's charge is serious, but plain. It is that Peter and the others acted in insincerity and not from personal conviction. Their withdrawal from table fellowship with Gentile believers was not prompted by any theological principle but by craven fear of a small pressure group.

If Paul had not taken his stand against Peter that day, either the whole Christian church would have drifted into a Jewish backwater and stagnated or there would have been a permanent rift between Gentile and Jewish Christianity. Paul's outstanding courage on that occasion in resisting Peter preserved both the truth of the gospel and the international fellowship of the church.

Courageous Confrontation

GALATIANS 2:14

> [14]When I saw that they were not acting in line with the truth of the gospel, I said to Cephas in front of them all, "You are a Jew, yet you live like a Gentile and not like a Jew. How is it, then, that you force Gentiles to follow Jewish customs?"

Paul made no attempt to hush up his dispute with Peter or arrange for a private discussion where the public and the press were excluded. The consultation in Jerusalem had been private, but the showdown in Antioch must be public. Peter's withdrawal from the Gentile believers had caused a public scandal; he had to be opposed in public too. It was just the kind of open head-on collision the church would seek at any price to avoid today.

Paul acted as he did out of a deep concern for the very principle Peter lacked. Paul knew that the theological principle at stake was no trivial matter. Peter and his associates were not acting "in line with the truth of the gospel." What is *the truth of the gospel*? It is the good news that we sinners, guilty and under the judgment of God, may be pardoned and accepted by his sheer grace, his free and unmerited favor, on the ground of his Son's death and not for any works or merits of our own. More briefly, the truth of the gospel is the doctrine of justification (which means acceptance before God) by grace alone through faith alone. Any deviation from this gospel Paul simply will not tolerate.

If God justifies Jews and Gentiles on the same terms, through simple faith in Christ crucified, and puts no difference between them, who are we to withhold our fellowship from Gentile believers unless they are circumcised? How dare we impose a condition on them which God does not impose? If God has accepted them, how can we reject them?

➤ Still today various Christian bodies and people repeat Peter's mistake. They refuse to have fellowship with professing Christian believers unless they have been baptized in a certain way, or unless they have been confirmed by certain officials, or unless their skin has a particular color, or unless they come out of a certain social drawer (usually the top one), and so on.

➤ All this is a grievous affront to the gospel. Justification is by faith alone; we have no right to add a particular mode of baptism or confirmation or any denominational, racial, or social conditions. God does not insist on these things before he accepts us into fellowship; so we must not insist on them either. The only barrier to communion with God, and therefore with each other, is unbelief, a lack of saving faith in Jesus Christ.

Justified by Faith

GALATIANS 2:15-16a

> [15]We who are Jews by birth and not sinful Gentiles [16]know
> that a person is not justified by the works of the law, but
> by faith in Jesus Christ.

Here the word *justified* occurs for the first time in Galatians.
Nobody has understood Christianity who does not understand this word. In this paragraph Paul unfolds the great doctrine of justification by faith. It is the good news that sinful
men and women may be brought into acceptance with God,
not because of their works but through a simple act of trust
in Jesus Christ.

Paul draws a contrast between the Judaizers' doctrine of justification by works of the law and the apostles' doctrine of justification through faith. By "the law" Paul means the sum total of
God's commandments, and by "the works of the law" he means
acts done in obedience to it. The Jews supposed they could be
justified by this means. So did the Judaizers, who professed to
believe in Jesus but wanted everybody to follow Moses as well.
If you do everything the law commands and refrain from everything the law forbids, you will make the grade.

Such was the position of the Jew and the Judaizer. It has been
the religion of the ordinary person both before and since. It is
the fundamental principle of every religious and moral system
in the world except New Testament Christianity. It is popular
because it is flattering. It tells us that if we will only try harder,
we will succeed in winning our own salvation.

But it is all a delusion. Nobody has ever been justified by the works of the law because nobody has ever perfectly kept the law. We may keep some of the law's requirements outwardly, but no one except Jesus Christ has ever kept them all. If we look into our hearts, read our thoughts, and examine our motives, we find that we have broken all God's laws.

The second alternative means of justification is "by faith in Jesus Christ." Jesus came into the world to live and to die. In his life, his obedience to the law was perfect. In his death, he suffered for our disobedience. He lived the only life of sinless obedience to the law that has ever been lived. On the cross he died for our lawbreaking, since the penalty for disobedience to the law was death.

All that is required of us to be justified, therefore, is to acknowledge our sin and helplessness, to repent of our self-assertion and self-righteousness, and to put our whole trust and confidence in Jesus Christ to save us. "Faith in Jesus Christ" is not intellectual conviction only, but personal commitment. It is an act of committal, not just assenting to the fact that Jesus lived and died, but running to him for refuge and calling on him for mercy.

A Triple Emphasis

GALATIANS 2:16b

> 16b So we, too, have put our faith in Christ Jesus that we may be justified by faith in Christ and not by the works of the law, because by the works of the law no one will be justified.

In verse 16 Paul makes an emphatic triple statement that is intended to leave us in no doubt about justification by faith.

The repetition is neither exact nor monotonous, for there is an ascending scale of emphasis—first general, then personal, and finally universal.

We have already seen that the first statement is general: "*a person* is not justified by the works of the law, but by faith in Jesus Christ" (v. 16a). Paul has nobody in particular in mind here; he is deliberately vague. Further, he says, "we know." He does not offer a tentative opinion but a dogmatic assertion. The plural "*we* know" means that the apostles Peter and Paul both know it; they are united in their conviction about the nature of the gospel.

The second statement is personal. Not only do "we know," but "we, too, have put our faith in Christ Jesus that we may be justified by faith in Christ." That is, our certainty about the gospel is more than intellectual; we have proved it personally in our own experience. This is an important addition. It shows that Paul is propounding a doctrine that he has put to the test. "We know it," he says, "and we have ourselves believed in Christ, in order to prove it."

The third statement is universal. The theological principle and the personal experience are now confirmed by Scripture. The apostle quotes the categorical statement of Psalm 143:2, as he will again in Romans 3:20. Whatever our religious upbringing, educational background, social status, or racial origin, the way of salvation is the same. None can be justified by works of the law; all must be justified through faith in Christ.

It is hard to find a more forceful statement of the doctrine of justification than this. It is insisted upon by the two leading apostles, confirmed from their own experience, and endorsed by the sacred

Scriptures of the Old Testament. With this threefold guarantee, we should accept the biblical doctrine of justification and not let our natural self-righteousness keep us from faith in Christ.

Christ Does Not Promote Sin

GALATIANS 2:17-18

> [17]But if, in seeking to be justified in Christ, we Jews find ourselves also among the sinners, doesn't that mean that Christ promotes sin? Absolutely not! [18]If I rebuild what I destroyed, then I really would be a lawbreaker.

Plain and pungent as Paul's exposition is, it was challenged in his day, and it is still being challenged today. So here he turns from exposition to argument. He tells us both the argument his critics used to try to overthrow his doctrine and the argument he used to overthrow their doctrine and to establish his. It is as though we hear them arguing with one another.

Paul's critics argued like this: "Your doctrine of justification through faith in Christ only, apart from the works of the law, is a highly dangerous doctrine. It fatally weakens a person's sense of moral responsibility. If we can be accepted through trusting in Christ, without any necessity to do good works, you are actually encouraging us to break the law, which is the heresy of antinomianism." People still argue like this today: "If God justifies bad people, what is the point of being good? Can't we do as we like and live as we please?"

Paul's first response to his critics is to deny their suggestion with hot indignation: "Absolutely not!" He specially denies the

added allegation that he was guilty of making Christ the agent
or author of sin. On the contrary, he says, "If after my justification I am still a sinner, it is my fault and not Christ's. I have
only myself to blame; no one can blame Christ."

Paul proceeds to refute his critics' argument. Their charge that
justification by faith encouraged a continuance in sin was ludicrous. They grossly misunderstood the gospel of justification. Justification is not a legal fiction in which our status is changed while
our character is left untouched. We are justified "in Christ." Our
justification takes place when we are united to Christ by faith.
And someone who is united to Christ is never the same person
again. It is not just our standing before God that has changed. *We*
are changed radically and permanently. For Paul, to talk of going
back to the old life, and even sinning as he pleases, is impossible.
He has become a new creation and begun a new life.

An Amazing Change

GALATIANS 2:19-21

> [19]For through the law I died to the law so that I might live
> for God. [20]I have been crucified with Christ and I no
> longer live, but Christ lives in me. The life I now live in the
> body, I live by faith in the Son of God, who loved me and
> gave himself for me.[21]I do not set aside the grace of God,
> for if righteousness could be gained through the law,
> Christ died for nothing!

Paul unfolds the amazing change that comes over a person who
is justified in Christ. He describes it in terms of a death and a

resurrection, both of which take place through union with Christ. It is *Christ's* death and resurrection we share in.

Perhaps now it is becoming clearer why a Christian who is justified in Christ is not free to sin. The death and resurrection of Christ are not only historical events but events in which his people have come to share through faith union with him. Once we have been united to Christ in his death, our old life is finished; it is ridiculous to suggest that we could ever go back to it. Besides, we have risen to a new life. In one sense we live this new life through faith in Christ. In another sense it is not we who live it at all, but Christ who lives it in us. Living in us, he gives us new desires for holiness, for God, for heaven. It is not that we cannot sin again. We can, but we do not want to. The whole tenor of our life has changed. Everything is different now because *we* are different.

If we insist that justification is by works and that we can earn our salvation by our own efforts, we set aside the grace of God (because if salvation is by works, it is not by grace) and we make Christ's death superfluous (because if salvation is our own work, then Christ's work was unnecessary).

Yet many people make the same mistakes as the Judaizers. They seek to commend themselves to God by their own works. They think it is noble to try to win their way to God and to heaven. But it is not noble; it is dreadfully ignoble. It is to deny both the nature of God and the mission of Christ. It is to refuse to let God be gracious. It is to tell Christ that he need not have bothered to die. If we are masters of our own destiny and can save ourselves, then both the grace of God and the death of Christ become unnecessary.

Galatians 2:11-21

....

DISCUSSION GUIDE

OPEN

When have you seen a conflict erupt between church leaders? What was it about, and how was it resolved (if it was)?

STUDY

Read Galatians 2:11–21.

1. Describe the situation that concerns Paul in this passage.

2. Taking into account Paul's previous meeting with Peter, James, and John in Jerusalem (Galatians 2:1-10), why would Paul have been especially incensed at Peter's behavior in Antioch?

3. What did Peter have to fear from the circumcision group?

4. Why do small pressure groups in the church arouse such fear in the majority and even in the leadership?

5. When have you given in to pressure and acted insincerely out of fear, rather than from personal conviction?

6. What made this issue worth the danger of a public confrontation?

7. In some Christian fellowships, believers hesitate to confront each other; in others they confront each other too quickly. What are the spiritual dangers of each approach?

8. How would keeping in mind what Paul called "the truth of the gospel" have affected the situations you recalled in questions 4 and 5?

9. Why would the gospel of God's grace bring down the accusation that Christ promotes sin (v. 17)?

10. Christians who are sure of their salvation can still be caught sinning. How does Paul deal with that uncomfortable fact?

11. Paul said that he no longer lives, but Christ lives in him (v. 20). How do you reconcile his words with the fact that Paul was still very much alive?

12. Why would Christ have "died for nothing" if righteousness could be gained through keeping the law (v. 21)?

APPLY

1. What pressures are you aware of—on yourself or within your Christian fellowship—to add conditions to the truth of the gospel?

4

Galatians 3:1-14
Faith and Works

❦

Foolishness Rebuked

GALATIANS 3:1-2

> [1]You foolish Galatians! Who has bewitched you? Before your very eyes Jesus Christ was clearly portrayed as crucified. [2]I would like to learn just one thing from you: Did you receive the Spirit by the works of the law, or by believing what you heard?

What have the Galatians done that leads Paul to complain of their senselessness and to ask if they have been bewitched? They have yielded to the teaching of the Judaizers. Having embraced the truth at the beginning (that sinners are justified by grace, in Christ, through faith), they have now adopted the view that circumcision and the works of the law are also necessary for justification.

The essence of Paul's argument is that their new position is a contradiction of the gospel. The reason for his astonishment at their folly is that before their very eyes Jesus Christ was "clearly portrayed as crucified." It is not just that Christ was portrayed before their eyes, but that he was portrayed before them *as crucified*.

The gospel is not a general instruction about the Jesus of history but a specific proclamation of Jesus Christ as crucified. Christ's work was completed on the cross, and the benefits of his crucifixion are forever fresh, valid, and available. If the Galatians had grasped the gospel of Christ crucified, that on the cross Christ did everything necessary for our salvation, they would have realized that the only thing required of them was to receive the good news by faith. To add good works to the work of Christ was an offense to his finished work.

Paul now exposes the senselessness of the Galatians. They should have resisted the spell of whoever was bewitching them. They knew perfectly well that the gospel is received by faith alone, since their own experience and the plain teaching of Scripture had told them so.

Paul assumes that the Galatian Christians have all received the Holy Spirit. His question is not whether they have received him but whether they received him by works or by faith. He assumes also that this is how their Christian life began. What he is asking concerns *how* they received the Spirit and so began the Christian life. There are two alternatives, which the apostle terms "by the works of the law" and "by believing what you heard." These are not two aspects of the same thing or interpretations of the same Christianity. They are contrary to one another. The law says "Do this"; the gospel says "Christ has done it all." The law requires works of human achievement; the gospel requires faith in Christ's achievement. The law makes demands and bids us obey; the gospel brings promises and bids us believe.

Consider Your Own Experience

GALATIANS 3:3-5

> [3]Are you so foolish? After beginning by means of the Spirit, are you now trying to finish by means of the flesh? [4]Have you experienced so much in vain—if it really was in vain? [5]So again I ask, does God give you his Spirit and work miracles among you by the works of the law, or by your believing what you heard?

Paul repeats his argument about how the Galatians began their Christian lives, but in a different way—not now from the point of view of *their* receiving the Spirit but from the point of view of *God* giving the Spirit: "Does God give you his Spirit and work miracles among you by the works of the law, or by your believing what you heard?" The verbs *give* and *work* do not necessarily refer to a continuous activity of God. It is more probable that they are timeless, referring still to Paul's visit when they received the Spirit, but now speaking of their experience from God's point of view. God gave them the Spirit (v. 5) and they received the Spirit (v. 2), not because they obeyed the law but because they believed the gospel.

They knew this fact because they had experienced it. Paul had come to Galatia and preached the gospel to them. He had publicly portrayed before their eyes Jesus Christ as crucified. They had heard the gospel and with the eye of faith had seen Christ displayed on his cross. They had believed the gospel. They had trusted in the Christ exhibited in the gospel. So they had received the Spirit. They had neither submitted to circumcision nor obeyed the law, nor even tried to. All they had done was to hear the gospel and believe, and the Spirit had been given to them.

These being the facts of their experience, Paul argues, it is ludicrous that "after beginning by means of the Spirit," they are now "trying to finish by means of the flesh." This is another way of saying that having begun with the gospel, they must not go back to the law, imagining that the law is needed to supplement the gospel. There is no way to improve on the gospel.

Gentiles Justified

GALATIANS 3:6-9

> [6]So also Abraham "believed God, and it was credited to him as righteousness."
>
> [7]Understand, then, that those who have faith are children of Abraham. [8]Scripture foresaw that God would justify the Gentiles by faith, and announced the gospel in advance to Abraham: "All nations will be blessed through you." [9]So those who rely on faith are blessed along with Abraham, the man of faith.

Paul's allusion to Abraham was a master stroke. His Judaizing opponents looked to Moses as their teacher. So Paul went centuries further back to Abraham himself. His quotation is from Genesis 15:6. Abraham was an old man and childless, but God had promised him a son, and indeed a seed or posterity. One day God took Abraham out of his tent, told him to look up at the sky and count the stars, and then said to him: "So shall your offspring be." Abraham believed God's promise, and it was credited to him as righteousness.

Consider carefully what happened. First, God made Abraham a promise. The promise of descendants was displayed before Abraham's eyes, much as the promise of forgiveness through Christ crucified was displayed before the eyes of the Galatians. Second, Abraham believed God. Despite the inherent improbability of the promise from the human point of view, Abraham cast himself on the faithfulness of God. Third, Abraham's faith was reckoned as righteousness. That is, he was accepted as righteous, by faith. He was justified not because he had done anything to deserve it or because he had been circumcised, or because he had kept the law (for neither circumcision nor the law had yet been given), but simply because he believed God.

Paul now links an earlier promise with this promise of God to Abraham. He quotes Genesis 12:3. The blessing is justification, the greatest of all blessings, for the verbs *to justify* and *to bless* are used as equivalents in verse 8. And the means by which the blessing would be inherited is faith. This was the only way that *Gentiles* could inherit Abraham's blessing, since Abraham was the father of the Jewish race. Perhaps the Judaizers were telling the Galatian converts that they should become the children of Abraham by circumcision. So Paul counters by saying that the Galatians were *already* the sons of Abraham, not by circumcision but by faith.

The Galatians should have known all this. They would never have fallen under the spell of the false teachers if they had kept

Christ crucified before their eyes. They should have realized at once that the Judaizers were contradicting the gospel of justification by faith alone. They should have known it, as we have seen, from their own experience and from the Scriptures of the Old Testament. We too should learn to test every theory and human teaching by the gospel of Christ crucified, especially as it is known to us from Scripture and from experience.

Under a Curse

GALATIANS 3:10

10For all who rely on the works of the law are under a curse, as it is written: "Cursed is everyone who does not continue to do everything written in the Book of the Law."

Paul quotes a verse from Deuteronomy that pronounces a solemn curse on everyone who fails to keep all the commandments of the law. To our sensitive modern ears these words sound crude and even harsh. We like to think of a God who blesses rather than a God who curses. Some people have tried to escape the dilemma by pointing out that Paul writes not of the curse of God but of the curse of the law. However, the law can never be isolated from God, for the law is God's law, the expression of his moral nature and will. What the law says, God says; what the law blesses, God blesses; and what the law curses, God curses.

There is no need to be embarrassed by these outspoken words. They express what Scripture everywhere tells us about God in relation to sin, namely, that no person can sin with impunity, for God is not a sentimental old Santa Claus but is the righteous

Judge of human beings. Disobedience always brings us under the curse of God and exposes us to the awful penalties of his judgment, to *curse* meaning not to *denounce* but actually to *reject*. So if the blessing of God brings justification and life, the curse of God brings condemnation and death.

Paul assumes the universality of sin. He shocks the Judaizers by asserting that the people who are under the curse are not just the ignorant, lawless Gentiles, as they imagine, but the Jews themselves as well.

We know this in our own experience. Sin is disregard for the laws of God. And all of us are lawless, for we have neither loved God with all our being nor loved our neighbor as ourselves. Having broken the laws of God, we have brought ourselves under the curse of the law, which is the curse of God. This is true of all people, not only the irreligious and the immoral, but Jews descended from Abraham, who were circumcised and in the covenant of God, yes and (to apply it to ourselves today) even baptized churchgoers too.

A Failed Alternative

GALATIANS 3:11-12

> [11]Clearly no one who relies on the law is justified before God, because "the righteous will live by faith." [12]The law is not based on faith; on the contrary, it says, "The person who does these things will live by them."

The apostle quotes twice from the Old Testament: "the righteous will live by faith" and "the person who does these things [that is, the requirements of the law] will live by them." Both statements come from Old Testament Scripture, the first from the prophets (Habakkuk 2:4), the second from the law (Leviticus 18:5). Both are therefore the word of the living God. Both say that a certain person "will live." In other words, both promise eternal life.

Despite these common features, the two statements describe two different roads to life. The first promises life to the believer, the second to the doer. The first makes faith the way of salvation, the second, works. The first says that only God can justify (because the function of faith is to trust God to do the work), the second implies that we can manage by ourselves. Which is true? Is a person justified by faith or by works? Do we receive eternal life by believing or by doing? Is salvation entirely and only by the free grace of God in Jesus Christ, or do we have some hand in it ourselves? And why does the Bible seem here to confuse the issue and teach both, when they appear to be contradictory?

It is true as an axiom that "the person who does these things will live by them." But nobody except Jesus has ever done them; therefore nobody can live by them. The dreadful function of the law is to condemn, not to justify. We may strive and struggle to keep the law and to do good works in the community or the church, but none of these things can deliver us from the curse of the law, which rests on the lawbreaker.

So this first supposed road to God leads to a dead end. There is neither justification nor life that way, but only darkness and death. We cannot help concluding, as Paul does: "Clearly no one who relies on the law is justified before God." The only way to escape the curse is not by our work but by his.

Christ Became a Curse for Us

Galatians 3:13-14

> [13]Christ redeemed us from the curse of the law by be-
> coming a curse for us, for it is written: "Cursed is everyone
> who is hung on a pole."[14]He redeemed us in order that the
> blessing given to Abraham might come to the Gentiles
> through Christ Jesus, so that by faith we might receive the
> promise of the Spirit.

Paul presents the second alternative for being justified before
God. It introduces Jesus Christ. It tells us that Jesus Christ has
done for us on the cross what we could not do for ourselves. He
has redeemed us, ransomed us, set us free from the awful condition of bondage that the curse of the law had brought us to.

Christ redeemed us "by becoming a curse for us." These are
astonishing words. In its context the phrase can mean only one
thing, for the "curse" of verses 10 and 13 is evidently the same
curse. The "curse of the law" that Christ redeemed us from must
be the curse resting on us for our disobedience. And he redeemed us from it by "becoming a curse" himself. The curse was
transferred from us to him. He took it voluntarily upon himself
in order to deliver us from it. This "becoming a curse" for us
explains the awful cry of dereliction, of God-forsakenness, he
uttered from the cross.

Paul now adds a scriptural confirmation of what he has just
said about the cross. Every criminal sentenced to death under the
Mosaic legislation and executed, usually by stoning, was then
fixed to a stake as a symbol of divine rejection. The fact that the

Romans executed by crucifixion rather than hanging makes no difference. To be nailed to a cross was equivalent to being hanged on a pole. So Christ crucified was recognized as having died under the divine curse. No wonder the Jews at first could not believe that Jesus was the Christ. How could Christ, the anointed of God, instead of reigning on a throne, hang on a stake? It was incredible to them. The fact that Jesus died hanging on a cross remained for Jews an insurmountable obstacle to faith, until they saw that the curse he bore was for *them*. He did not die for his own sins; he became a curse *for us*.

Does this mean that everybody has been redeemed from the law's curse through the sin-bearing, curse-bearing cross of Christ? No, for it is "by faith" that we "receive the promise of the Spirit." It was in Christ that God acted for our salvation, and so we must be in Christ to receive it. We are not saved by a distant Christ, who died hundreds of years ago and lives millions of miles away, but by an existential Christ, who, having died and risen again, is now our contemporary. By faith we can be "in him," personally and vitally united to him today.

Galatians 3:1-14

....

DISCUSSION GUIDE

OPEN

In what areas of life are you tempted to try to earn God's favor by your good actions?

STUDY

Read Galatians 3:1-14.

1. What words and phrases reveal Paul's attitude toward the Galatians?

2. Twice Paul calls the Galatian Christians "foolish" (vv. 1, 3). In what senses is it foolish to add works to the gospel of Christ?

3. In artwork Christ is portrayed in many ways: teaching crowds, working alongside Joseph in the carpenter shop, praying in Gethsemane, welcoming children, walking on water. Why would Paul choose to focus on portraying Christ as crucified?

4. After beginning our Christian lives by faith, most of us at one time or other imitate the Galatians and fall into relying on our own efforts. Why do you think this happens?

5. To the Judaizers, who were misleading the Galatian Christians, Abraham was a hero and patriarch. How does Paul turn the tables and use Abraham as an example of faith instead of law keeping?

6. What do we have in common with Abraham?

7. The ugly words *curse* and *cursed* appear often in this passage. What justifies Paul's use of such language?

8. Why is there a curse hanging over those who try to rely on observing the law?

9. The "curse of the law" that Christ redeemed us from must be the curse resting on us for our disobedience (v. 10). And he redeemed us from it by "becoming a curse" himself. He voluntarily took our curse upon himself in order to deliver us from it. What does it mean to you that Christ became a curse for us?

10. What are some differences between law and faith?

11. In your own experience, what does it mean to "live by faith"?

12. What are some obstacles to living by faith?

Apply

1. Consider ways that you might have fallen into trying to please God or earn his favor by your own efforts. How does this passage encourage you to examine your heart?

2. Think of someone you know who is struggling with self-effort. How can you help restore that person to trust in Christ?

5

Galatians 3:15-29
The Gift of the Law

❧

The Promise to Abraham

GALATIANS 3:15-18

[15]Brothers and sisters, let me take an example from everyday life. Just as no one can set aside or add to a human covenant that has been duly established, so it is in this case. [16]The promises were spoken to Abraham and to his seed. Scripture does not say "and to seeds," meaning many people, but "and to your seed," meaning one person, who is Christ. [17]What I mean is this: The law, introduced 430 years later, does not set aside the covenant previously established by God and thus do away with the promise. [18]For if the inheritance depends on the law, then it no longer depends on the promise; but God in his grace gave it to Abraham through a promise.

The conclusion Paul is leading to is that the Christian religion is the religion of Abraham and not Moses, of promise and not

law, and that Christians today enjoy the promise God made to
Abraham centuries ago. But in this passage, having contrasted
these two kinds of religion, he shows the relation between them.
We cannot set Abraham and Moses, the promise and the law,
against each other, accepting one and rejecting the other. If God
is the author of both, he must have had some purpose for both.
What then is the relation between them?

Paul divides his subject into two parts. Verses 15-18 are neg-
ative, teaching that the law did not annul the promise of God.
Verses 19-22 will be positive, teaching that the law illumined
God's promise and actually made it indispensable.

Paul begins with an everyday human example taken from the
realm of human promises, not a business contract but a will,
what we call a person's "last will and testament." The wishes and
promises expressed in a will are unalterable. And if a *person*'s will
cannot be set aside or added to, much more are the promises of
God immutable.

God promised an inheritance to Abraham and his posterity.
God said that in Abraham's seed all the families of the earth
would be blessed. God's purpose was not just to give the land of
Canaan to the Jews, but to give salvation (a spiritual inheritance)
to believers who are in Christ.

God's promise was free and unconditional. There were no
strings attached. The promise is still in force today, for it has never
been rescinded. God has never annulled or modified his will.

"What I mean is this," Paul says. "The law, introduced 430 years
later, does not set aside the covenant previously established by
God and thus do away with the promise." If the Judaizers were

right, our Christian inheritance (justification) is given to those
who keep the law, and if it is by the law, it is no longer by promise.

But God has not gone back on his promise. It is as binding
as a human will; indeed, more so. So every sinner who trusts in
Christ crucified for salvation, quite apart from any merit or good
works, receives the blessing of eternal life and thus inherits the
promise of God made to Abraham.

Why the Law?

GALATIANS 3:19-20

[19]Why, then, was the law given at all? It was added because
of transgressions until the Seed to whom the promise referred had come. The law was given through angels and
entrusted to a mediator. [20]A mediator, however, implies
more than one party; but God is one.

We can almost hear the indignant objection of the Judaizers: "If
it is only through faith that a person is in Christ and becomes a
beneficiary of God's promise to Abraham, what is the point of
the law? Your theology so fuses Abraham and Christ that you
squeeze out Moses and the law altogether. There's no room for
the law in your gospel."

Paul had his answer ready. The Judaizers misunderstood and
misrepresented his position. He was far from declaring the law
unnecessary, for he was quite clear that it had an essential part
to play in the purpose of God. The function of the law was not
to bestow salvation, however, but to convince people of their
need of it.

"Why, then, was the law given at all?" It was "because of transgressions." The law's main work was to expose sin. It is the law which turns *sin* into *transgression*, showing it up for what it is, a breach of the holy law of God. The law was intended to make plain the sinfulness of sin as a revolt against the will and authority of God. And it was added "until the Seed to whom the promise referred had come." The law looked ahead to Christ, Abraham's seed, as the Person through whom transgression would be forgiven.

The rest of verse 19 and verse 20 are acknowledged to be difficult. They have been variously interpreted. The apostle is probably emphasizing the inferiority of the law to the gospel. The activity of angels in connection with the giving of the law is mentioned several times in Scripture. The "mediator" is doubtless Moses. So when God gave the law, he spoke through angels and through Moses. But when God spoke the gospel to Abraham, he did it directly, and that is probably the meaning of the phrase "God is one."

Law Versus Promises?

GALATIANS 3:21-22

> [21]Is the law, therefore, opposed to the promises of God? Absolutely not! For if a law had been given that could impart life, then righteousness would certainly have come by the law. [22]But Scripture has locked up everything under the control of sin, so that what was promised, being given through faith in Jesus Christ, might be given to those who believe.

The law cannot justify us. Then how is it possible to create a harmony between the law and the promise? Only by seeing that we inherit the promise because we cannot keep the law, and that our inability to keep the law makes the promise all the more desirable, indeed indispensable. Scripture holds every sinner in prison for his or her sins, "so that what was promised, being given through faith in Jesus Christ, might be given to those who believe."

The Judaizers held falsely that the law annuls the promise and supersedes it; Paul teaches the true function of the law, which is to confirm the promise and make it indispensable.

With a breadth of vision that leaves us far behind, the apostle Paul brings together Abraham, Moses, and Jesus Christ. In eight short verses he spans about two thousand years. He surveys practically the whole Old Testament landscape. He presents it like a mountain range whose highest peaks are Abraham and Moses and whose Everest is Jesus Christ. He shows how God's promise to Abraham was confirmed by Moses and fulfilled in Christ. He teaches the unity of the Bible, especially the Old and New Testaments.

Some people think of the Bible as a tangled undergrowth of unrelated ideas, full of contradictions. In fact, one of the chief glories of the Bible is its coherence. The whole Bible, from Genesis to Revelation, tells the story of God's sovereign purpose of grace, his master plan of salvation through Christ.

After God gave the promise to Abraham, he gave the law to Moses. Why? Because he had to make things worse before he could make them better. The law exposed sin, provoked sin, condemned sin. The purpose of the law was to lift the lid off our respectability and disclose what we are really like underneath—sinful, rebellious, guilty, under the judgment of God, and helpless to save ourselves.

The law must still be allowed to do its God-given duty today. The contemporary church tends to soft-pedal sin and judgment. We must never bypass the law and come straight to the gospel. To do so is to contradict the plan of God in biblical history.

Not until the law has bruised and smitten us will we admit our need of the gospel to bind up our wounds. Not until the law has arrested and imprisoned us will we pine for Christ to set us free. Not until the law has driven us to despair of ourselves will we ever believe in Jesus.

Locked Up by the Law

GALATIANS 3:23-24

> [23]Before the coming of this faith, we were held in custody under the law, locked up until the faith that was to come would be revealed. [24]So the law was our guardian until Christ came that we might be justified by faith.

God's purpose for our spiritual pilgrimage is that we should pass through the law into an experience of the promise. The tragedy is that so many people separate law and promise by wanting one without the other. Some try to go to Jesus without first meeting Moses. They want to skip the Old Testament, to inherit the promise of justification in Christ without the prior pain of condemnation by the law. Others go to Moses and the law to be condemned, but they stay in this unhappy bondage. They are still living in the Old Testament. Their religion is a grievous yoke, hard to bear. They have never gone to Christ to be set free.

Paul sets out to depict both these spiritual stages. Verses 23-24 describe what we were under the law, while verses 25-29 will describe what we are in Christ.

The apostle uses two vivid similes in which the law is likened first to a prison in which we were held captive, and then to a tutor whose discipline was harsh and severe. The verbs "held in custody" and "locked up" both emphasize that God's law and commandments keep us confined so that we cannot escape. The "guardian" is more literally a tutor, usually a slave, whose duty was to lead a boy to and from school and to generally watch his conduct. He was not the boy's teacher so much as his disciplinarian. He is usually depicted in ancient drawings with a rod or cane in his hand.

Like a jailer, the law has thrown us into prison; like a strict tutor, it rebukes and punishes us for our misdeeds. But, thank God, he never meant this oppression to be permanent. He gave the law in his grace in order to make the promise more desirable. So to both descriptions of our bondage Paul adds a time reference. "Before the coming of this faith," we were held captive by the law, "until the faith that was to come would be revealed." And the law was our tutor "until Christ came." The oppressive work of the law was temporary. It was ultimately intended not to hurt but to bless. Its purpose was to shut us up in prison until Christ should set us free, or to put us under tutors until Christ should make us his children.

Children of God

GALATIANS 3:25-27

> [25]Now that this faith has come, we are no longer under a guardian.

²⁶So in Christ Jesus you are all children of God through faith, ²⁷for all of you who were baptized into Christ have clothed yourselves with Christ.

Paul's phrase "Now that this faith has come" underlines that what we are is quite different from what we were.

God is no longer our Judge who through the law has condemned and imprisoned us. God is no longer our Tutor who through the law restrains and chastises us. God is now our Father who in Christ has accepted and forgiven us. We no longer fear him, dreading the punishment we deserve; we love him with deep devotion as child to parent. We are neither prisoners awaiting the final execution of our sentence nor minor children under the restraint of a tutor, but children of God and heirs of his glorious kingdom, enjoying the status and privileges of grownup children.

Our status as children of God is not in ourselves; it is "in Christ." The doctrine of God as a universal Father was not taught by Christ or by his apostles. God is the universal Creator who brought all things into existence, and he is the universal King who rules and sustains all that he has made. But he is the Father only of our Lord Jesus Christ and of those he adopts into his family through Christ. If we want to be the children of God, then we must be "in Christ Jesus . . . through faith."

Our baptism visibly sets forth this union with Christ. Paul cannot possibly mean that the act of baptism itself unites a person to Christ. We must give him credit for a consistent theology. His whole letter is devoted to the theme that we are justified through faith, not circumcision. It is inconceivable that Paul should now substitute baptism for circumcision and teach that we are in

Christ by baptism! The apostle clearly makes *faith* the means of our union with Christ. He mentions faith five times in this paragraph, but baptism only once. Faith secures the union; baptism signifies it outwardly and visibly. Thus in Christ, by faith inwardly and by baptism outwardly, we are all children of God.

One in Christ

GALATIANS 3:28-29

> [28]There is neither Jew nor Gentile, neither slave nor free, nor is there male and female, for you are all one in Christ Jesus. [29]If you belong to Christ, then you are Abraham's seed, and heirs according to the promise.

In Christ we belong not only to God as his children but to each other as brothers and sisters. And we belong to each other in such a way as to render of no account the things that normally distinguish us, such as race, rank, and sex.

First, *there is no distinction of race.* God called Abraham and his descendants in order to entrust to them his unique self-revelation. But when Christ came, God's promise was fulfilled that in Abraham's seed all the families of the earth would be blessed. This includes all nations of every race, color, and language. We are equal in our need of salvation, equal in our inability to earn or deserve it, and equal in the fact that God offers it to us freely in Christ.

Second, *there is no distinction of rank.* Nearly every society in the history of the world has developed its class or caste system. Circumstances of birth, wealth, privilege, and education have divided people from one another. But in Christ snobbery is prohibited and class distinctions are rendered void.

Third, *there is no distinction of sex.* This remarkable assertion of the equality of the sexes was centuries ahead of its time. Women were nearly always despised in the ancient world, even in Judaism, and not infrequently exploited and ill-treated. But here Paul—supposed by many to be antifeminist—makes the assertion that in Christ male and female are one and equal.

Of course every person belongs to a certain race and nation, has been nurtured in a particular culture, and is either male or female. When we say that Christ has abolished these distinctions, we do not mean that they cease to exist but that they do not matter. They are still there, but they no longer create any barriers to fellowship. By the grace of God we resist the temptation to despise one another or patronize one another, for we know ourselves to be "all one in Christ Jesus."

We have seen that in Christ we belong to God and to each other. In Christ we also belong to Abraham. We take our place in the noble historical succession of faith whose outstanding representatives are listed in Hebrews 11. No longer do we feel ourselves to be waifs and strays, without any significance in history, or bits of useless flotsam drifting on the tide of time. Instead, we find our place in the unfolding purpose of God. We are the spiritual seed of our father Abraham, who lived and died four thousand years ago, for in Christ we have become heirs of the promise that God made to him.

Galatians 3:15-29

....

Discussion Guide

Open

How would you describe your attitude toward God's law?

Study

Read Galatians 3:15-29.

1. Trace the steps of Paul's argument that the introduction of law through Moses (the "mediator" of v. 19) does not supersede God's promise to Abraham.

2. Why is a will an appropriate metaphor for the point Paul is making?

3. How is Christ foreshadowed in God's promise to Abraham?

4. God's promise to Abraham was made a very long time ago. How do modern-day Christians still participate in it?

5. Why must we choose between relying on the law and relying on the promise?

6. If God's law can't save anyone, why did God give it to humanity?

7. How does law lead us toward Christ?

8. What are some comparisons between being in prison and trying to earn God's favor by following his law?

9. How do people resist the "tutor" that is trying to lead them to Christ?

10. What difference does it make for you to see yourself as a child of God?

11. What difference does it make for you to see other Christians as children of God?

12. Differences of race, social standing, and gender obviously exist among Christians. What should be Christians' attitude toward these natural differences?

Apply

1. How did God's law lead you to Christ?

2. In what ways do you find yourself being drawn back into bondage to law?

3. Where would you like to see oneness in Christ more of a reality, and what can you do to encourage it?

6

Galatians 4:1-31
Children of God

❦

Underage Heirs

GALATIANS 4:1-3

> [1]What I am saying is that as long as an heir is underage, he is no different from a slave, although he owns the whole estate. [2]The heir is subject to guardians and trustees until the time set by his father. [3]So also, when we were underage, we were in slavery under the elemental spiritual forces of the world.

In Galatians 3 the apostle Paul surveyed two thousand years of Old Testament history. In particular, he showed the relation among three of the great figures of biblical history—Abraham, Moses, and Jesus Christ. Now Paul will rehearse the same history again, contrasting our condition under the law with our condition in Christ, and making an impassioned appeal about the Christian life. His sequence of thought can be summarized:

"Once we were slaves. Now we are children. How then can we turn back to the old slavery?"

Under the law, Paul says, we were like an underage heir during childhood or minority. This child is under restraint. He has no liberty. Because he is the heir, he is in fact the lord, but while he is a child, he is no better than a slave. We were in the same condition. Even in Old Testament days, before Christ came and when we were under the law, we were heirs—heirs of the promise God made to Abraham. But we had not yet inherited the promise. We were like children during the years of their minority; our childhood was a form of slavery.

What was this slavery? We know that it was slavery to the law. But here the law is equated with "the elemental spiritual forces of the world." In the ancient world elemental spirits were often associated with the physical elements (earth, fire, air, and water) or with the heavenly bodies (the sun, moon, and stars), which control the seasonal festivals observed on earth.

Paul was not suggesting that the law was an evil design of Satan. He has told us that the law was given to Moses by God, not Satan, and mediated through angels—good spirits, not bad. What Paul means is that the devil took this good thing (the law) and twisted it to his own evil purpose in order to enslave men and women.

God intended the law to reveal sin and to drive us to Christ; Satan uses it to reveal sin and to drive us to despair. God meant the law as an interim step to our justification; Satan uses it as the final step to our condemnation. God meant the law to be a steppingstone to liberty; Satan uses it as a dead end, deceiving us into supposing that there is no escape from its bondage. But there is "a time set by his father" for the heir to come into his own. That time arrived in all its fullness when Christ entered the world.

Adopted by God

GALATIANS 4:4-7

> [4]But when the set time had fully come, God sent his Son, born of a woman, born under the law, [5]to redeem those under the law, that we might receive adoption to sonship. [6]Because you are his sons, God sent the Spirit of his Son into our hearts, the Spirit who calls out, "*Abba*, Father." [7]So you are no longer a slave, but God's child; and since you are his child, God has made you also an heir.

Humanity's bondage under the law continued for about thirteen hundred years. But at last the fullness of time arrived—the date set by the Father when the children should attain their majority, be freed from their guardians, and inherit the promise.

When this fullness of time had come, God did two things.

First, "God sent his Son." Notice that God's purpose was both to *redeem* and to *adopt*, not just to rescue from slavery but to make slaves into his own children. The one who God sent to accomplish our redemption was perfectly qualified to do so. He was God's Son. He was also born of a human mother, so that he was human as well as divine, the one and only God-man. And he was born "under the law," that is, of a Jewish mother, into the Jewish nation, subject to the Jewish law. He succeeded where all others before and since have failed: he perfectly fulfilled the righteousness of the law. So the divinity of Christ, the humanity of Christ, and the righteousness of Christ uniquely qualified him to be our Redeemer.

Second, "God sent the Spirit." Note the trinitarian reference. First, God sent his Son into the world; second, he sent his Spirit into our hearts. And, entering our hearts, the Spirit immediately began to cry "Abba! Father!" *Abba* is the word Jesus used in intimate prayer to God. God sent his Son that we might have the *status* of being his children, and he sent his Spirit that we might have an *experience* of it. This comes through the affectionate, confidential intimacy of our access to God in prayer, in which we find ourselves assuming the attitude and using the language not of slaves but of children.

The indwelling presence of the Holy Spirit is the precious privilege of all God's children. There is no need to recite some formula or strive after some experience or fulfill some extra condition. Paul says clearly that *if* we are God's children, and *because* we are God's children, God has sent his Spirit into our hearts. And the way he assures us that we are his children is not by some spectacular gift or sign, but by the quiet inward witness of the Spirit as we pray.

How Can We Turn Back?

GALATIANS 4:8-11

⁸Formerly, when you did not know God, you were slaves to those who by nature are not gods. ⁹But now that you know God—or rather are known by God—how is it that you are

turning back to those weak and miserable forces? Do you wish to be enslaved by them all over again? [10]You are observing special days and months and seasons and years! [11]I fear for you, that somehow I have wasted my efforts on you.

Again Paul contrasts what once we were with what we have become. But this time the contrast is painted in terms of our knowledge of God. Our bondage was to evil spirits, owing to our ignorance of God; our status as God's children consists in the knowledge of God, knowing him and being known by him in the intimacy of personal communion.

Now comes the apostle's appeal. His argument is this: "If you were a slave and are now a child, if you did not know God but have now come to know him and to be known by him, how can you turn back again to the old slavery? How can you allow yourself to be enslaved by the very elemental spirits Jesus Christ has rescued you from?" Your religion has degenerated into an external formalism. It is no longer the free and joyful communion of children with their Father; it has become a dreary routine of rules and regulations. Paul fears that all the time and trouble he has spent over them has been wasted.

It is not impossible to turn back to the old life; the Galatians had done it. But it is preposterous to do so. It is a fundamental denial of what we have become, of what God has made us if we are in Christ.

The way for us to avoid the Galatians' folly is to heed Paul's words. Let God's Word keep telling us who and what we are in Christ. One of the great purposes of daily Bible reading, meditation, and prayer is to get ourselves correctly oriented. We need to say to ourselves, "Once I was a slave, but God has made me his child and put the Spirit of his Son into my heart. How can I turn back to the old slavery? Once I did not know God, but now I know him and have come to be known by him. How can I turn back to the old ignorance?"

By the grace of God we must determine to remember what we once were and determine never to return to it, to remember what God has made us and to conform our lives to it. If only we remember these things, we will have an increasing desire within us to live accordingly, to be what we are, namely, children of God set free by Christ.

Become Like Me

GALATIANS 4:12-16

> [12]I plead with you, brothers and sisters, become like me, for I became like you. You did me no wrong. [13]As you know, it was because of an illness that I first preached the gospel to you, [14]and even though my illness was a trial to you, you did not treat me with contempt or scorn. Instead, you welcomed me as if I were an angel of God, as if I were Christ Jesus himself. [15]Where, then, is your blessing of me now? I can testify that, if you could have done so, you would have torn out your eyes and given them to me. [16]Have I now become your enemy by telling you the truth?

So far we have been listening to Paul the apostle, Paul the theologian, Paul the defender of the faith, but now we are hearing Paul the man, Paul the pastor, Paul the passionate lover of souls.

Paul pleads with the Galatians to "become like me." In the context this appeal can mean only one thing. Paul longed for them to become like him in his Christian faith and life, to be delivered from the evil influence of the false teachers, and to share his convictions about the truth as it is in Jesus, about the liberty with which Christ has made us free. He wanted them to become like himself in his Christian freedom. All Christians should be able to say something like this to unbelievers, namely, that we are so satisfied with Jesus Christ, with his freedom, joy, and salvation, we want other people to become like us.

"For I became like you," Paul reminds them. When he came to them in Galatia, he did not keep his distance or insist on his own dignity, but became like them. He put himself in their place and identified himself with them. Although he was a Jew, he became like the Gentiles they were. As we seek to win other people for Christ, if they are to become one with us in Christian conviction and experience, we must first become one with them in Christian compassion.

Paul has no complaint about the Galatians' former treatment of him. He reminds them that he first preached the gospel to them "because of an illness." Whatever the disease was, it evidently had unpleasant and unsightly symptoms. But the Galatians neither despised nor rejected Paul. Instead, "you welcomed me as if I were an angel of God, as if I were Christ Jesus himself." This is an extraordinary expression. It is another indication of Paul's self-conscious apostolic authority. In receiving Paul the Galatians quite rightly received him as Christ, for they recognized him as an apostle or delegate of Christ.

But that was some time ago. Now a complete about-face has taken place. The one they had received as God's angel, as God's Son, they now regard as their enemy! Why? Simply because he has been telling them some painful truths, rebuking them, scolding them, expostulating with them for deserting the gospel of grace and turning back again to bondage.

There is an important lesson here. An apostle's authority does not cease when the apostle begins to teach unpopular truths. We cannot be selective in our reading of the apostolic doctrine of the New Testament. The apostles of Jesus Christ have authority in everything they teach, whether or not we happen to like it.

My Dear Children

GALATIANS 4:17-20

> [17]Those people are zealous to win you over, but for no good. What they want is to alienate you from us, so that you may have zeal for them. [18]It is fine to be zealous, provided the purpose is good, and to be so always, not just when I am with you.[19]My dear children, for whom I am again in the pains of childbirth until Christ is formed in you, [20]how I wish I could be with you now and change my tone, because I am perplexed about you!

Paul draws a contrast between the attitude of the false teachers toward the Galatians and his own attitude toward them. He seems to accuse the false teachers of flattering the Galatians insincerely. In order to win them to their perverted gospel, the false teachers fawned on them and fussed over them. Their real motive was to *alienate* the Galatians from the apostles so that the false teachers would receive the honor and attention.

Paul's attitude to the Galatians is quite different from that of the false teachers. He calls them "my dear children" and likens himself to their mother. The point of the mother metaphor is not to illustrate the Galatians' dependence on Paul but rather his travail for them. He is not satisfied that Christ lives in them; he longs to see Christ *formed* in them, to see them transformed into the image of Christ.

The difference between Paul and the false teachers should now be clear. The false teachers were seeking *themselves* to dominate the Galatians; Paul longed for *Christ* to be formed in them. They had a selfish eye to their own prestige and position; Paul was prepared to sacrifice himself for them, to be in travail until Christ was formed in them.

From this paragraph we may learn the reciprocal relationship that should exist between a Christian congregation and their pastor. The people's attitude toward their minister should be determined not by the minister's appearance or by their own private theological ideas, but by the minister's loyalty to the apostolic message. If the minister is faithful in teaching what the apostles taught, a godly congregation will humbly receive the message and submit to it. And a Christian minister's attitude should resemble that of Paul, not that of the Judaizers. The minister should be preoccupied with the people's spiritual progress and care nothing for personal prestige or advantage.

What should matter to the people is not the pastor's appearance but whether *Christ* is speaking through the pastor. And what should matter to the pastor is not the people's approval but whether *Christ* is formed in them. The church needs people who, in listening to their pastor, listen for the message of Christ, and pastors who, in laboring among the people, look for the image of Christ. Only when pastor and people thus keep their eyes on Christ will their mutual relations keep healthy, profitable, and pleasing to almighty God.

Children of the Free Woman

GALATIANS 4:21-31

[21]Tell me, you who want to be under the law, are you not aware of what the law says? [22]For it is written that Abraham had two sons, one by the slave woman and the other by the free woman. [23]His son by the slave woman was born according to the flesh, but his son by the free woman was born as the result of a divine promise.

[24]These things are being taken figuratively: The women represent two covenants. One covenant is from Mount Sinai and bears children who are to be slaves: This is Hagar. [25]Now Hagar stands for Mount Sinai in Arabia and corresponds to the present city of Jerusalem, because she is in slavery with her children. [26]But the Jerusalem that is above is free, and she is our mother. [27]For it is written:

"Be glad, barren woman,
    you who never bore a child;
  shout for joy and cry aloud,
    you who were never in labor;

because more are the children of the desolate woman
than of her who has a husband."

[28]Now you, brothers and sisters, like Isaac, are children
of promise. [29]At that time the son born according to the
flesh persecuted the son born by the power of the Spirit. It
is the same now. [30]But what does Scripture say? "Get rid
of the slave woman and her son, for the slave woman's son
will never share in the inheritance with the free woman's
son." [31]Therefore, brothers and sisters, we are not children
of the slave woman, but of the free woman.

Paul's message is addressed to "you who want to be under the law."
There are many such people today whose religion is legalistic.
They imagine that the way to God is by the observance of rules.
There are even professing Christians who turn the gospel into law.
Paul meets and refutes such people on their own ground.

The historical background. The Jews boasted that they were
descended from Abraham, the father and founder of their race.
Paul argues that true descent from Abraham is not physical but
spiritual. Abraham's true children are not those with an impec-
cable Jewish genealogy but those who believe as Abraham believed and obey as Abraham obeyed.

This double descent from Abraham, the false being literal and
physical, the true being figurative and spiritual, Paul sees illus-
trated in Abraham's two sons, Ishmael and Isaac. Both had
Abraham as their father, but they were born of different mothers.
Ishmael was born into slavery, while Isaac was born into freedom.
Ishmael was born according to nature, but Isaac was born against

nature, supernaturally, through an exceptional promise of God. Each of us is either an Ishmael or an Isaac, by nature a slave or by the grace of God set free.

The allegorical argument. God established the old covenant through Moses and the new covenant through Christ. God's people under the old covenant were the Jews, but his people under the new covenant are Christian believers. Both are "Jerusalem," but the old covenant people of God, the Jews, are "the present city of Jerusalem," the earthly city, while the new covenant people of God, the Christian church, are "the Jerusalem that is above," the heavenly city. Hagar and Sarah, the mothers of Abraham's two sons, stand for the two covenants (the old and the new) and the two Jerusalems (the earthly and the heavenly).

The personal application. The treatment Isaac got from his half-brother Ishmael is the treatment that Isaac's spiritual descendants will get from Ishmael's spiritual descendants. And the treatment that Isaac got from his father Abraham is the treatment that we must expect from God. The persecution of the true church, of Christian believers who trace their spiritual descent from Abraham, is not always by the world but by our half-siblings, religious people, the nominal church.

Although Isaac endured the scorn of his half-brother Ishmael, Isaac became heir of his father Abraham and received the inheritance. So we must seek to be like Isaac, not like Ishmael. We must put our trust in God through Jesus Christ. For only in Christ can we inherit the promises, receive the grace, and enjoy the freedom of God.

Galatians 4:1-31

....

DISCUSSION GUIDE

OPEN

When and why have you had an especially strong awareness that you are a child of God?

STUDY

Read Galatians 4:1-31.

1. Identify all the examples of symbolism you note in this passage.

2. What are the differences between the way a slave on an estate and the child of the estate owner would relate to the master (owner)?

3. Think of differences in conversation together, physical bearing toward each other, attitude toward the estate, and how time in each other's presence is spent. How does this parallel your relationship with God as his child?

4. In verse 9 we are told that we not only know God but are known by God. Do you find it comforting? unsettling? cheering?

5. In what sense(s) did Paul want the Galatians to become like him (v. 12)?

6. What was the contrast between what Paul and his companions wanted for the Galatians and what the false teachers wanted?

7. Why do you think Paul had refused to give up on the Galatian church?

8. How does Paul share in the love and suffering of Christ for the Galatians?

9. How does Paul use the history of Abraham's two sons, Ishmael and Isaac, to illustrate the supremacy of promise over law?

10. How does Paul demonstrate that physical descent from Abraham is not enough to make someone a child of God?

11. Why does conflict persist between followers of the old and new covenants?

12. In what ways have you seen, or even experienced firsthand, conflict and misunderstanding between legalistic Christians and those who know God's grace and are trusting his promises?

13. In what areas of your life are you enjoying the freedom of a child of God?

APPLY

1. How do you usually respond to legalism?

2. How can "free" Christians guard against their own kind of self-righteousness, feeling superior to legalists?

7

Galatians 5:1-15
True and False Religion

❦

Stand Firm in Freedom

GALATIANS 5:1-4

¹It is for freedom that Christ has set us free. Stand firm, then, and do not let yourselves be burdened again by a yoke of slavery.

²Mark my words! I, Paul, tell you that if you let yourselves be circumcised, Christ will be of no value to you at all. ³Again I declare to every man who lets himself be circumcised that he is obligated to obey the whole law. ⁴You who are trying to be justified by the law have been alienated from Christ; you have fallen away from grace.

Paul portrays our former state as slavery, Jesus Christ as liberator, conversion as an act of emancipation, and the Christian life as a life of freedom. As the entire letter and the immediate context make plain, this freedom is not primarily freedom from sin but rather from the law. What Christ has done is not so much to set our *will* free from the bondage of sin as to set our *conscience* free from the guilt of sin. The Christian freedom Paul describes is freedom of conscience, freedom from the tyranny of the law, the dreadful struggle to keep the law, with a view to winning the favor of God. It is the freedom of acceptance with God and of access to God through Christ. Since "Christ has set us free," we must "stand firm" in that freedom and not let ourselves "be burdened again by a yoke of slavery."

From the general theme of freedom we come to the precise issue of circumcision. The false teachers in the Galatian churches were saying that Christian converts had to be circumcised. We might think this a trivial matter. Why did Paul make so much fuss and bother about it? Because of its doctrinal implications. As the false teachers were pressing it, circumcision was neither a physical operation nor a ceremonial rite, but a theological symbol. It stood for a particular type of religion, namely, salvation by good works in obedience to the law.

In three sentences Paul warns the Galatians of the serious results of their receiving circumcision: "Christ will be of no value to you at all. . . . You . . . have been alienated from Christ," and "you have fallen away from grace." More simply, to add circumcision is to lose Christ; to seek to be justified by the law is to fall from grace.

You cannot have it both ways. It is impossible to receive Christ, thereby acknowledging that you cannot save yourself, and then receive circumcision, thereby claiming that you can. You must choose between a religion of law and a religion of grace, between Christ and circumcision. You cannot add circumcision (or anything else, for that matter) to Christ as necessary to salvation, because Christ is sufficient for salvation in himself. If you add anything to Christ, you lose Christ. Salvation is in Christ alone by grace alone through faith alone.

Waiting in Faith

GALATIANS 5:5-6

> [5]For through the Spirit we eagerly await by faith the righteousness for which we hope. [6]For in Christ Jesus neither circumcision nor uncircumcision has any value. The only thing that counts is faith expressing itself through love.

The pronoun changes from *you* to *we*. Paul has been addressing his readers and warning them of the danger of falling from grace. Now he includes himself and describes true believers, evangelical believers, who stand in the gospel of grace. He makes two statements about faith.

First, "we eagerly await by faith the righteousness for which we hope." Our expectation for the future, which our justification brings, is spending eternity with Christ in heaven. For this future salvation we wait. We do not *work* for it; we *wait* for it by faith. We do not strive anxiously to secure it or imagine that we have to earn it by good works. Final glorification in heaven is as free a gift as our initial justification. So by faith, trusting only in Christ crucified, we wait for it.

Second, "in Christ Jesus . . . the only thing that counts is faith expressing itself through love." Again Paul denies the false teaching. When a person is in Christ, nothing more is necessary. Neither circumcision nor uncircumcision can improve our standing before God. All that is necessary in order to be accepted with God is to be in Christ, and we are in Christ by faith.

Does this emphasis on faith in Christ mean that we can live and act as we please? Is the Christian life so completely a life of faith that good works and obedience to the law do not matter? No. Paul is very careful to avoid giving any such impression. It is "through the Spirit" that we wait for the hope of righteousness. The Christian life is not only a life of faith; it is a life in the Spirit. The Holy Spirit who indwells us produces good works of love. And what counts is "faith expressing itself through love." It is not that works of love are added to faith as a second and subsidiary ground of our acceptance with God, but that the faith which saves is a faith which works, a faith which issues in love.

An Interrupted Race

GALATIANS 5:7-9

> [7]You were running a good race. Who cut in on you to keep you from obeying the truth? [8]That kind of persuasion does not come from the one who calls you. [9]"A little yeast works through the whole batch of dough."

Paul loved to liken the Christian life to a race in the arena. Notice that "running a good race" is not just believing the truth (as if Christianity were nothing but orthodoxy), nor just behaving well (as if it were only moral uprightness), but "obeying the truth," applying belief to behavior. Only the one who obeys the truth is an integrated Christian. What we believe and how we behave must be consistent. Our creed is expressed in our conduct; our conduct is derived from our creed.

The Galatians had begun the Christian race, and at first they ran well. They believed the truth that Christ had set them free, and they obeyed it, enjoying the liberty Christ had given them. But someone had hindered them; an obstacle had been thrown on the track to deviate them from the path. False teachers had contradicted the truth they had first believed. As a result they had forsaken Christ and fallen from grace.

The false teachers had persuaded the Galatians to abandon the truth of the gospel, but this work of persuasion was not from the God who had called them. For God had called them in grace, whereas the false teachers were propagating a doctrine of merit. The false teachers' message was inconsistent with the Galatians' call.

Paul uses the common proverb, "A little yeast works through the whole batch of dough." That is, the error of the false teachers was spreading in the Christian community until the whole church was becoming contaminated. So because of the cause and effect of the false teaching, because it was not from God and because its influence was spreading, Paul was determined to resist it.

The Proof of Persecution

Galatians 5:10-12

[10]I am confident in the Lord that you will take no other view. The one who is throwing you into confusion, whoever that may be, will have to pay the penalty. [11]Brothers and sisters, if I am still preaching circumcision, why am I still

being persecuted? In that case the offense of the cross has
been abolished. [12]As for those agitators, I wish they would
go the whole way and emasculate themselves!

Paul is quite sure that error is not going to triumph, but that the
Galatians will come to a better mind. He knows that the false
teachers, however exalted their rank, will fall under the judgment
of God. Indeed, Paul is so concerned about the damage the false
teachers are doing that he even expresses the wish that they
castrate themselves like heathen priests. To our ears his sentiment sounds coarse and malicious. We may be quite sure,
however, that it was due neither to an intemperate spirit nor to
a thirst for revenge, but to his deep love for the people of God
and the gospel of God.

It seems that these teachers had dared even to claim Paul as
a champion of their views. They were spreading the rumor that
Paul also preached and advocated circumcision. The apostle
flatly denies it and goes on to give evidence of the falsity of their
claim. They were preaching circumcision; he was preaching
Christ and the cross. To preach circumcision is to tell sinners
that they can save themselves by their own good works; to
preach Christ crucified is to tell them that only Christ can save
them through the cross. The message of circumcision is in-
offensive and flattering; the message of Christ crucified is offensive to human pride. So to preach circumcision is to avoid
persecution, while to preach Christ crucified is to invite it.

Now since he was being persecuted, Paul argues that he was
not preaching circumcision. On the contrary, he was preaching
Christ crucified, and the stumbling block of the cross had not

been removed. It was the false teachers who were pressing the Galatians to be circumcised in order to avoid persecution for the cross of Christ.

Through the centuries of the Christian church, until and including today, Christian preachers who refuse to distort or dilute the gospel of grace have had to suffer for their faithfulness. If we preach this gospel, we will arouse ridicule and opposition. Only if we preach "circumcision," human merit and sufficiency, will we escape persecution and become popular.

Christianity will not allow us to sit on the fence or live in a haze. It urges us to be definite and decisive, and in particular to choose between circumcision—human merit—and Christ crucified.

Service Through Love

GALATIANS 5:13

> [13]You, my brothers and sisters, were called to be free. But do not use your freedom to indulge the flesh; rather, serve one another humbly in love.

Having asserted that we have been called to liberty, Paul immediately sets himself to define the freedom we have been called to in order to clear it of misconceptions and to protect it from irresponsible abuse. In brief, it is freedom from the awful bondage of having to merit the favor of God; it is not freedom from all controls.

In the language of the apostle Paul, "the flesh" is not what clothes our bony skeleton, but our fallen human nature, which we inherited from our parents and they inherited from theirs, and which is twisted with self-centeredness and therefore prone to sin. We are not to use our Christian freedom to indulge this flesh. Our freedom in Christ is not to be used as a pretext for self-indulgence.

Christian freedom is freedom *from* sin, not freedom *to* sin. It is an unrestricted liberty of approach to God as his children, not an unrestricted liberty to wallow in our own selfishness.

Christian freedom is no more freedom to do as I please irrespective of the good of my neighbor than it is freedom to do as I please in the indulgence of my flesh. It is freedom to approach God without fear, not freedom to exploit my neighbor without love.

Indeed, far from having liberty to ignore, neglect, or abuse our fellow human beings, we are commanded to love them, and through love to serve them. We are not to use them as if they were things to serve us; we are to respect them as persons and give ourselves to serve them. Through love we are even to literally become each other's *slaves*, sacrificing our good for theirs, not theirs to ours.

It is a remarkable paradox. For from one point of view Christian freedom is a form of slavery—not slavery to our flesh but to our neighbor. We are free in relation to God, but slaves in relation to each other.

The Law of Love

GALATIANS 5:14-15

> [14]For the entire law is fulfilled in keeping this one command: "Love your neighbor as yourself." [15]If you bite and devour each other, watch out or you will be destroyed by each other.

The apostle does not say that if we love one another we can safely *break* the law of God in the interests of love, but that if we love one another we will *fulfill* God's law, because the whole law is summed up in this one command, "Love your neighbor as yourself."

Our Christian freedom from the law that Paul emphasizes concerns our relationship to God. It means that our acceptance depends not on our obedience to the law's demands but on faith in Jesus Christ, who bore the curse of the law when he died. It certainly does not mean that we are free to disregard or disobey the law.

On the contrary, although we cannot gain acceptance by keeping the law, yet once we have been accepted we will keep the law out of love for him who has accepted us and has given us his Spirit to enable us to keep it. In New Testament terminology, although our justification depends not on the law but on Christ crucified, our sanctification consists in the fulfillment of the law.

If we love one another we will serve one another, and if we serve one another we will not "bite and devour each other" in malicious talk or action. For biting and devouring are destructive, while love is constructive; love serves.

Christian liberty is freedom not to indulge the flesh but to control the flesh, freedom not to exploit our neighbor but to serve our neighbor, freedom not to disregard the law but to fulfill the law. Everyone who has been truly set free by Jesus Christ expresses liberty in these three ways, first in self-control, next in loving service of our neighbor, and third in obedience to the law of God.

Galatians 5:1-15

....

Discussion Guide

Open

Different branches of the Christian church practice various ceremonies and observe various scruples according to conscience. How do you discern whether a custom or practice has become elevated to something necessary for salvation?

Study

Read Galatians 5:1-15.

1. What does Paul express concern about in this passage?

2. What words and phrases throughout this passage indicate what it means to be free?

3. Most people value their freedom very highly. Why would anyone need to be warned to stand fast and avoid submitting to slavery?

4. How could Jesus Christ ever be said to be "of no value" (v. 2)?

5. In verse 4, how do you interpret Paul's phrase "fallen away from grace"?

6. If we have been declared righteous in Christ, why would Paul say that we still hope for it (v. 5)?

7. In verses 7-12, the contrast is between "the one who is throwing you into confusion" (the false teacher) and Paul himself, who is teaching the truth of God. How does the image of a race highlight the problem?

8. How could Paul be so sure that the "persuasion" of the false teachers (v. 10) was not from God, who had called the Galatians?

9. What is the significance of the "yeast" in the "dough" (v. 9)?

10. What was Paul falsely being accused of, and how does he respond (vv. 11-12)?

11. Describe some ways in which the misuse of Christian freedom could lead to self-indulgence.

12. How could freedom degenerate to Christians attacking one another (v. 15)?

13. Why is "love your neighbor as yourself" an appropriate summary of God's law?

Apply

1. Where are you in the greatest danger of imposing a requirement like the Judaizers?

2. How are you inclined to indulge yourself in the name of your freedom in Christ?

8

Galatians 5:16–6:5
Loving One Another

✦

Flesh Versus Spirit

GALATIANS 5:16-18

¹⁶So I say, walk by the Spirit, and you will not gratify the desires of the flesh. ¹⁷For the flesh desires what is contrary to the Spirit, and the Spirit what is contrary to the flesh. They are in conflict with each other, so that you are not to do whatever you want. ¹⁸But if you are led by the Spirit, you are not under the law.

Each time Paul writes of liberty, he adds a warning that it can very easily be lost. Some relapse from liberty into bondage; others turn their liberty into license. He has emphasized that true Christian liberty expresses itself in self-control, loving service of our neighbor, and obedience to the law of God. The question now is, how are these things possible? And the answer is, by the Holy Spirit. He alone can keep us truly free.

Paul presents the Holy Spirit as our Sanctifier who alone can oppose and subdue our flesh, enable us to fulfill the law so that we are delivered from its harsh dominion, and cause the fruit of righteousness to grow in our lives. True, it is Christ who sets us free. But without the continuing, directing, sanctifying work of the Holy Spirit our liberty is bound to degenerate into license.

Paul identifies a Christian conflict in which the combatants are called "the flesh" and "the Spirit." By "the flesh" Paul means what we are by nature and inheritance, our fallen condition. By "the Spirit" he seems to mean the Holy Spirit himself, who renews and regenerates us, first giving us a new nature and then remaining to dwell in us. More simply, we may say that "the flesh" stands for what we are by natural birth, "the Spirit" what we become by new birth. These two, the flesh and the Spirit, are in sharp opposition to each other.

Some teachers maintain that the Christian has no inner conflict or civil war because (they say) our flesh has been eradicated our old nature is dead. This passage contradicts such a view. Certainly, as we learn to walk in the Spirit, the flesh becomes increasingly subdued. But the flesh and the Spirit remain, and the conflict between them is fierce and unremitting. We may go further and say that this is a specifically Christian conflict. We do not deny that there is such a thing as moral conflict in non-Christian people, but it is fiercer in Christians because we possess two natures—flesh and Spirit—in irreconcilable antagonism.

So Paul has been emphasizing that life in Christ is liberty. And the enjoyment of Christian liberty depends on the Holy Spirit.

The Acts of the Flesh

GALATIANS 5:19-21

> [19]The acts of the flesh are obvious: sexual immorality, im-
> purity and debauchery; [20]idolatry and witchcraft; hatred,
> discord, jealousy, fits of rage, selfish ambition, dissensions,
> factions [21]and envy; drunkenness, orgies, and the like. I
> warn you, as I did before, that those who live like this will
> not inherit the kingdom of God.

"The acts of the flesh" are obvious to all. The flesh itself, our
old nature, is secret and invisible; but its works, the words
and deeds in which it erupts, are public and evident. What
are they?

Paul has already mentioned "the desires of the flesh" (v. 16).
We may think of these as connected with our bodily appetites,
but Paul's meaning is much wider than this. For him "the desires of the flesh" are all the sinful desires of our fallen nature.
Now his ugly catalog of "the works of the flesh" puts this beyond
question. The list is not exhaustive, for he adds the phrase "and
the like." But those he includes belong to at least four realms:
sex, religion, society, and drink.

First, the realm of sex: "sexual immorality, impurity and de-
bauchery." These three words are sufficient to show that all sexual
offenses, whether public or private, whether between the married
or the unmarried, whether "natural" or "unnatural," are to be
classed as "acts of the flesh."

Second, the realm of religion: "idolatry and witchcraft." It is
important to see that idolatry is as much a work of the flesh as

immorality, and that thus the works of the flesh include offenses against God as well as against our neighbor or ourselves.

Third, the realm of society: Paul now gives us eight examples of the breakdown of personal relationships: "hatred, discord, jealousy, fits of rage, selfish ambition, dissensions, factions and envy."

Fourth, the realm of drink: "drunkenness, orgies."

To this list of the acts of the flesh in the realms of sex, religion, society, and drink, Paul adds a solemn warning. "I warn you, as I did before [when he was with them in Galatia], that those who live like this [the verb refers to habitual practice rather than an isolated lapse] will not inherit the kingdom of God." Since God's kingdom is a kingdom of godliness, righteousness, and self-control, those who indulge in the acts of the flesh will be excluded from it. For such works give evidence that they are not in Christ. And if they are not in Christ, then they are not Abraham's offspring and cannot "inherit the kingdom of God."

The Fruit of the Spirit

GALATIANS 5:22-23

> [22]But the fruit of the Spirit is love, joy, peace, forbearance, kindness, goodness, faithfulness, [23]gentleness and self-control. Against such things there is no law.

Here we have a cluster of nine Christian graces that seem to portray Christians' attitude toward God, toward other people, and toward ourselves.

"Love, joy, peace." This is a triad of general Christian virtues. Yet they seem primarily to concern our attitude toward God, for as Christians our first love is love for God, our chief joy is our joy in God, and our deepest peace is our peace with God.

Next, "forbearance, kindness, goodness." These are social virtues directed toward others rather than toward God. *Forbearance* is longsuffering toward those who aggravate or persecute us. *Kindness* is a matter of disposition, while *goodness* is a matter of words and actions.

The third triad is "faithfulness, gentleness, self-control." *Faithfulness* appears to describe the reliability of a Christian person. *Gentleness* is that humble meekness that Christ exhibited. Both are aspects of self-mastery or *self-control.*

All these qualities are "the fruit of the Spirit." They are the natural produce that appears in the lives of Spirit-led Christians. No wonder Paul adds "against such things there is no law." The function of law is to curb, to restrain, and to deter, and here no deterrent is needed.

It should now be even clearer that "the flesh" and "the Spirit" are in active conflict with one another. They are pulling in opposite directions "so that you are not to do whatever you want" (v. 17). A Christian says, "My new nature hungers for God, for godliness and for goodness. I want to be good and to do good." That is the language of every regenerate believer. "But," we have to add, "by myself, even with these new desires, I cannot do what I want to do. Why not? Because of sin that dwells within me."

This is the Christian conflict—fierce, bitter, and unremitting. It is a conflict in which we cannot be victorious by ourselves.

Is that the whole story? Is this all Christianity offers—an experience of continuous defeat? Indeed, it is not. If we were left to ourselves, we could not do what we want to do; instead, we would succumb to the desires of our old nature. But if we "walk by the Spirit," then we "will not gratify the desires of the flesh" (v. 16). We will still experience them, but we will not indulge them. On the contrary, we will bear "the fruit of the Spirit."

Walk by the Spirit

GALATIANS 5:24-25

24Those who belong to Christ Jesus have crucified the flesh with its passions and desires. 25Since we live by the Spirit, let us keep in step with the Spirit.

The crucifixion Paul speaks of here is not the same as the one he speaks of in other places, where he says that we are crucified with Christ by faith union with him. Here we are the ones who have taken action to do the crucifying.

To "take up one's cross" was Jesus' vivid figure of speech for self-denial. Now Paul takes the metaphor to its logical conclusion. We must not only take up our cross and walk with it, but actually see that the execution takes place. We are to take the flesh, our willful and wayward self, and (metaphorically speaking) nail it to the cross.

A Christian's rejection of the old nature is to be *pitiless*. Crucifixion was not administered to nice or refined people; it was reserved for the worst criminals, which is why it was such a shameful thing for Jesus Christ to be crucified. If we are to crucify our flesh, it is plain that the flesh is not something respectable to be treated with courtesy and deference, but something so evil that it deserves no better fate than to be crucified.

Our rejection of the old nature will be *painful*. Crucifixion was an intensely painful form of execution. And which of us does not know the acute pain of inner conflict when we renounce the pleasures of sin?

The rejection of our old nature is to be *decisive*. Once nailed to the cross, the criminal was left there to die. So, Paul says, if we have crucified the flesh, we must leave it there to die. We must renew every day our ruthless and uncompromising rejection of sin.

We turn now to the attitude we are to adopt toward the Holy Spirit. It is to be "led by the Spirit" (v. 18) and to "walk by the Spirit" (v. 16) or "keep in step with the Spirit" (v. 25). The Spirit does the leading, but we do the walking.

As our leader, the Holy Spirit takes the initiative. He asserts his desires against those of the flesh and forms holy and heavenly desires within us. He puts this gentle pressure on us, and we must yield to his direction and control.

But it is a great mistake to suppose that our whole duty lies in passive submission to the Spirit's control, as if all we had to do was to surrender to his leading. On the contrary, we are ourselves to walk, actively and purposefully, in the right way. To walk by the Spirit is to deliberately walk along the path or according to the line that the Holy Spirit lays down. It is not enough to yield passively to the Spirit's control; we must also walk actively in the Spirit's way.

Reciprocal Relationships

GALATIANS 5:26–6:2

> [26]Let us not become conceited, provoking and envying each other.
>
> [1]Brothers and sisters, if someone is caught in a sin, you who live by the Spirit should restore that person gently. But watch yourselves, or you also may be tempted. [2]Carry each other's burdens, and in this way you will fulfill the law of Christ.

"Let us not become conceited, provoking and envying each other." These are very instructive words because they show that our conduct to others is determined by our opinion of ourselves. When we are conceited, our relationships with other people are bound to be poisoned.

If we regard ourselves as superior to other people, we challenge them, for we want them to know and feel our superiority. If we regard them as superior to us, we envy them. In both cases our attitude is due to our having such a fantasy opinion of ourselves that we cannot bear rivals. Very different is that love which is the fruit of the Spirit, which Christians exhibit when they are walking by the Spirit. The Holy Spirit has opened their eyes to see both their own sin and unworthiness, and also the importance and value of other people in the sight of God.

The command to "carry each other's burdens" assumes that we all have burdens and that God does not mean us to carry them alone. Of course we can cast all our burdens on Christ, but one of the ways he bears our burdens is through human friendship. To be a burden bearer is a great ministry. It is something that every Christian should and can do. It is a natural consequence of walking by the Spirit.

Paul gives us a particular example of burden-bearing: "if someone is caught in a sin, you who live by the Spirit should restore that person gently." If we detect somebody doing something wrong, we are not to stand by doing nothing. Nor are we to despise or condemn the sinner, report the sinner to the minister, or gossip about the sinner. No, we are to *restore* that person. And it is only those "who live by the Spirit" who should attempt the restoration. It should be done *gently*—gentleness being one of the fruits of the Spirit. Paul adds that we are to be watchful, lest we also are tempted. This suggests that gentleness toward others is born of a sense of our own weakness and tendency to sin.

If we walk by the Spirit, we will love one another more; if we love one another more, we will bear one another's burdens; and if we bear one another's burdens, we will not shrink from seeking to restore a believer who has fallen into sin. If we obey this apostolic instruction as we should, much unkind gossip will be avoided, serious backsliding will be prevented, the good of the church will be advanced, and the name of Christ will be glorified.

Test Our Actions

GALATIANS 6:3-5

> [3]If anyone thinks they are something when they are not, they deceive themselves. [4]Each one should test their own actions. Then they can take pride in themselves alone,

without comparing themselves to someone else, [5]for each
one should carry their own load.

Paul's implication is that if we do not or will not bear one another's burdens, it is because we think we are above it. We would
not demean ourselves to such a thing; it would be beneath our
dignity. Again it is apparent that our conduct to others is gov-
erned by our opinion of ourselves. Just as we provoke and envy
other people when we have self-conceit, so when we think we
are "something," we decline to bear others' burdens.

The truth is that we are not *something*; we are *nothing*. Is this
an exaggeration? Not when the Holy Spirit has opened our eyes
to see ourselves as we are, rebels against the God who made us
in his image, deserving nothing at his hand but destruction.
When we realize and remember this, we will not compare ourselves favorably with other people, nor will we decline to serve
them or bear their burdens.

Even when we are Christians, redeemed by God through
Jesus Christ, we will still not compare ourselves with others.
These comparisons are odious and dangerous, as the apostle goes
on to say. Instead of scrutinizing our neighbors and comparing
ourselves with them, we are to "test [our] own actions," for we
will have to carry our "own load." That is, we are responsible to
God for our work and must one day give an account of it to him.

We are to bear one another's burdens that are too heavy for a
person to bear alone. But there is one burden we cannot share—
indeed do not need to, because it is a pack light enough for every
person to carry—and that is our responsibility to God on the
day of judgment. On that day you cannot carry my pack, and I
cannot carry yours. We must each individually answer to God.

Galatians 5:16–6:5

....

Discussion Guide

Open

For some Christians the Holy Spirit is the vaguest member of the Trinity. For others he is vital to their experience in Christ. How do you see the Holy Spirit in his involvement with your spiritual life?

Study

Read Galatians 5:16–6:5.

1. What are the causes and some practical results of the Christian's inner moral conflict?

2. All Christians have the unhappy experience of discovering that we want God's will but have failed to do it. When we get that insight into ourselves, what are some typical ways we respond, and why?

3. Two ways of living are described in Galatians 5:19-25. What is the root of the contrast between the two?

4. Consider the areas of sex, religion, society, and drink. Why is each especially vulnerable to corruption by the sinful nature?

5. Reflect on the character qualities called "the fruit of the Spirit" in Galatians 5:22-23. What is significant about the fact that they are called "fruit," in contrast with the "acts" of the sinful nature?

6. Why is crucifixion (5:24) an apt description of what must happen to the sinful nature?

7. How do the fruit of the Spirit make us Christlike in our attitude toward God? toward other people? toward ourselves?

8. Why would conceit lead us to provoke and envy each other (5:26)?

9. How would you identify a person who is living by the Spirit (6:1)?

10. What temptations would accompany becoming involved in the restoration of a Christian who has fallen into sin (6:1)?

11. What are some examples of burdens that Christians can and should carry for each other?

12. When Paul speaks of bearing one another's burdens, which fruits of the Spirit is he calling on believers to exercise?

13. When have other Christians helped bear your burdens?

APPLY

1. What burdens of your own do you need to share with others?

2. Whose burdens can you help carry today?

9

Galatians 6:6-18
Sowing and Reaping

❦

Two-Way Fellowship

GALATIANS 6:6

⁶Nevertheless, the one who receives instruction in the word should share all good things with their instructor.

Whether the instruction given is private, in a school where converts are being prepared for baptism, or to a whole congregation by their pastor, the principle is the same, that the one who is taught the word should help to support the teacher. So a minister may expect to be supported by the congregation. The one who sows the good seed of God's Word should reap a livelihood.

Some people find this embarrassing. But the principle is emphasized many times in Scripture. If the principle is properly applied, it contains its own safeguards. Nevertheless, we ought to consider its two possible abuses.

Although few ministers could be described as overpaid, the popular image of the Christian minister (at least in the Western world) seems to be that the job is undemanding and secure. Some Christian ministers are tempted to laziness. Often nobody supervises their work. So it is not unknown for ministers to grow slack. It is understandable, therefore, that Paul renounced his own right to get his living from the gospel and preached free of any charge, earning his living as a tentmaker. And yet the scriptural principle is clear, that the minister should be set free from secular wage earning in order to be devoted to the study and the ministry of the Word and to the care of the flock.

If the principle of the congregation paying the minister may encourage the minister to be lazy and neglectful, it may also tempt the congregation to try to control the minister. Some congregations exercise tyranny and almost blackmail the pastor into preaching what they want to hear. Of course it is wrong for a minister to yield to such pressure, but it is also wrong for a congregation to put the minister in this predicament.

The minister shares spiritual things with the congregation, and they share material things with the minister. The right relationship between teacher and taught, or minister and congregation, is one of partnership and fellowship.

Two Logical Harvests

GALATIANS 6:7-8

> [7]Do not be deceived: God cannot be mocked. A man reaps what he sows. [8]Whoever sows to please their flesh, from the flesh will reap destruction; whoever sows to please the Spirit, from the Spirit will reap eternal life.

Paul likens the Christian's life to a farmstead where the flesh and the Spirit are two fields in which we may sow seed. The harvest we reap depends on *where* and on *what* we sow.

This is a vitally important and neglected principle of holiness. We are not helpless victims of our nature, temperament, and environment. On the contrary, what we become depends largely on how we behave. Our character is shaped by our conduct.

To "sow to please the flesh" is to pander to it and indulge it instead of crucifying it. The seeds we sow are largely thoughts and deeds. Every time we allow our mind to harbor a grudge, nurse a grievance, entertain an impure fantasy, or wallow in self-pity, we are sowing to please the flesh. Every time we linger in bad company whose influence we know we cannot resist, every time we lie in bed when we ought to be praying, every time we view pornography, every time we take a risk which strains our self-control, we are sowing to please the flesh.

By contrast, to "sow to please the Spirit" is the same as to "walk by the Spirit" (Galatians 5:16) and to "keep in step with the Spirit" (Galatians 5:25). Again, the seeds we sow are our thoughts and deeds. By the material we read, the company we keep, and the leisure occupations we pursue, we can be sowing to please the Spirit. In addition, we are to foster disciplined habits of devotion in private and in public, in daily prayer and Bible reading, and in worship with the Lord's people on the Lord's Day. All this is sowing to the Spirit; without it there can be no harvest of the Spirit, no fruit of the Spirit.

Paul distinguishes between the two harvests as well as between the two sowings. The results are only logical. If we sow to the flesh, we "will reap destruction." A process of moral decay will set in. We will go from bad to worse until we finally perish. If, on the other hand, we sow to the Spirit, we "will reap eternal life." A process of moral and spiritual growth will begin. Communion with God (which is eternal life) will develop now until in eternity it becomes perfect.

Holiness is a harvest; whether we reap it or not depends on what and where we sow. If we want to reap a harvest of holiness, we must avoid sowing to the flesh and must keep sowing to the Spirit. It is another way of saying (as in Galatians 5) that we must crucify the flesh and walk by the Spirit. There is no other way of growing in holiness.

A Sure Harvest

Galatians 6:9-10

> [9] Let us not become weary in doing good, for at the proper time we will reap a harvest if we do not give up. [10] Therefore, as we have opportunity, let us do good to all people, especially to those who belong to the family of believers.

Active Christian service is tiring, exacting work. We are tempted to become discouraged, to slack off, even to give up. So the apostle gives us this incentive: he tells us that doing good is like sowing seed. If we persevere in sowing, then "at the proper time we will reap a harvest if we do not give up."

If the farmer tires of sowing and leaves half the field unsown, there will be only half a crop. It is the same with good deeds. If we want a harvest, then we must finish the sowing and be patient. We cannot expect to sow and reap on the same day.

If the sowing is the doing of good works, what is the harvest? Paul does not tell us; he leaves us to guess. But patiently doing good in the church or community always produces good results. It may bring comfort, relief, or assistance to people in need. It may lead a sinner to repentance and so to salvation. It may help to arrest the moral deterioration of society and even to make it a sweeter and more wholesome place to live. It may increase people's respect for what is beautiful, good, and true. And it will bring good to the doer as well—not salvation, for this is a free gift of God, but some reward in heaven for faithful service, which will probably take the form of yet more responsible service.

"Therefore," since the sowing of good seed results in a good harvest, "as we have opportunity [and this earthly life is full of such opportunity], let us do good to all people, and especially to those who belong to the family of believers." These are our brothers and sisters in the family of God. Our kin may claim our first loyalty, but Christian charity must never stop there. Jesus said we are to love and serve not only our friends but our enemies. Persistent well-doing is a characteristic of the true Christian. It is a characteristic so indispensable that it will be taken as evidence of saving faith on the Judgment Day.

We must expect to reap what we sow. Therefore, if we want to reap a good harvest, we must sow, and keep sowing, good seed. Then, in due time, we are sure to reap a bountiful harvest of good.

Outward or Inward?

GALATIANS 6:11-12

¹¹See what large letters I use as I write to you with my own hand!

¹²Those who want to impress people by means of the flesh are trying to compel you to be circumcised. The only reason they do this is to avoid being persecuted for the cross of Christ.

Christianity is fundamentally not a religion of external ceremonies but something inward and spiritual, in the heart. But the Judaizers concentrated on something outward, namely, on circumcision. Paul is outspoken about why. They "want to impress people by means of the flesh." The Judaizers elevated circumcision to an ordinance of central importance, insisting that without it nobody could be saved. But how could an outward and bodily operation secure the salvation of the soul or be an indispensable condition of salvation? It was plainly ridiculous.

What matters primarily is not whether a person has been circumcised (or baptized) or not, but whether the person has been born again and is now a new creation. Circumcision was, and baptism is, an outward sign and seal of this. The circumcision of the body symbolized the circumcision of the heart. Similarly, baptism with water symbolizes the baptism of the Holy Spirit. It is a lamentable tragedy when we become so topsy-turvy in our thinking that we substitute the sign for the thing signified, magnify a bodily ceremonial at the expense of a change of heart, and make circumcision or baptism instead of the new creation the way of salvation. Circumcision and baptism are things of the *flesh*, outward and visible ceremonies performed by people; the new creation is a birth of the Spirit, an inward and invisible miracle performed by God.

Throughout history God's people have tended to repeat this same mistake. They have debased a religion of the heart into a superficial, outward show, and God has repeatedly sent his messengers to reprove them and to recall them to a spiritual and inward religion. Much contemporary "churchianity" is the same—dry, dull, dismal, and dead, largely an external show. It is natural to fallen humanity to decline from the real, the inward, and the spiritual, and to fabricate a substitute religion that is easy and comfortable because its demands are external and ceremonial only. But outward things matter little in comparison with the new creation or the new birth.

This is not to say that the bodily and the external have no place, for what is in the heart needs to be expressed through the lips, and what is inward and spiritual in religion needs to have some outward expression. But the essence is the inward; outward forms are valueless if inward reality is lacking.

Human or Divine?

GALATIANS 6:13-16

> [13]Not even those who are circumcised keep the law, yet they want you to be circumcised that they may boast about your circumcision in the flesh. [14]May I never boast except in the cross of our Lord Jesus Christ, through which the world has been crucified to me, and I to the world. [15]Neither

circumcision nor uncircumcision means anything; what counts is the new creation. [16]Peace and mercy to all who follow this rule—to the Israel of God.

Circumcision was not only an outward and bodily ritual; it was also a *human* work, performed by one human being on another. More than that, as a religious symbol, circumcision committed people to keep the law. The Judaizers' idea of the way of salvation was that the death of Christ was insufficient; we still have to merit the favor and forgiveness of God by our own good works.

Paul vigorously challenges this teaching. He even impugns the motives of the Judaizers and calls their bluff. They cannot seriously believe that salvation is a reward for obedience to the law, because "not even those who are circumcised keep the law." They know that salvation cannot be earned. Why then do they still insist on meritorious works? As Paul has already stated, it is "to avoid being persecuted for the cross of Christ."

What is it about the cross of Christ that angers the world and stirs them up to persecute those who preach it? Just this: Christ died on the cross for us sinners, becoming a curse for us. So the cross tells us some very unpalatable truths about ourselves, that we are sinners under the righteous curse of God's law and that we cannot save ourselves. Christ bore our sin and curse precisely because we could gain release from them in no other way. Nothing in history or in the universe cuts us down to size like the cross.

Of course people do not like this. They resent the humiliation of seeing themselves as God sees them and as they really are. They prefer their comfortable illusions. So they steer clear of the cross. They construct a Christianity without the cross, which relies for salvation on their works and not on those of Jesus Christ. They do not object to Christianity so long as it is not the faith of Christ crucified.

The attitude of the apostle Paul was totally at variance with these views. "May I never boast except in the cross of our Lord Jesus Christ, through which the world has been crucified to me, and I to the world." The cross for Paul was not something to escape but the object of his boasting. We cannot boast in ourselves and in the cross simultaneously. If we boast in ourselves and in our ability to save ourselves, we will never boast in the cross and in the ability of Christ crucified to save us.

We have to choose. Only if we have humbled ourselves as hell-deserving sinners will we give up boasting of ourselves, fly to the cross for salvation, and spend our days glorying in the cross.

The Marks and the Grace

GALATIANS 6:17-18

> [17]From now on, let no one cause me trouble, for I bear on my body the marks of Jesus.
> [18]The grace of our Lord Jesus Christ be with your spirit, brothers and sisters. Amen.

Doubtless the "marks of Jesus" Paul speaks of were wounds he had received while being persecuted for Jesus' sake. In other places he refers to numerous beatings, and some of these sufferings may already have been endured before this letter. Certainly he had already been stoned and left for dead in Lystra, one of the Galatian cities. The wounds his persecutors had inflicted on him and the permanent scars they left behind—these were the "marks of Jesus." Greek slaves were branded to show ownership, and it is possible that Paul had this practice in mind. He was a slave of Jesus; he had received his branding in his persecutions.

Paul's marks of persecution were the ground of his plea: "From now on, let no one cause me trouble." Paul longed to be left alone by the false teachers. He had not avoided persecution for the cross of Christ. On the contrary, he carried wounds on his body, which designated him a true slave and a faithful devotee of Jesus Christ.

Paul began his letter to the Galatians with his customary salutation of grace (Galatians 1:3) and went on to express his astonishment that the Galatians were deserting the God who had called them in the grace of Christ (Galatians 1:6). The whole letter is dedicated to the theme of God's grace, his unmerited favor to sinners.

Now Paul ends on the same note. The authentic characteristic of the gospel is "the grace of our Lord Jesus Christ," and of the gospel preacher "the marks of Jesus." This is so for all God's people. Paul bore the marks of Jesus on his body and the grace of Jesus in his spirit. And he desired his readers to have the same, for they were his "brothers and sisters" in the family of God.

So we have Christ through his apostles to teach us, Christ through his cross to save us, and Christ through his Spirit to sanctify us. This in a nutshell is the message of the letter to the Galatians and indeed of Christianity itself. It is all included in the letter's last words: "The grace of our Lord Jesus Christ"—his grace through his apostles, his cross, and his Spirit—"be with your spirit, brothers and sisters. Amen."

Galatians 6:6-18

....

DISCUSSION GUIDE

OPEN

When have you seen "good sowing" produce "good reaping"?

STUDY

Read Galatians 6:6–18.

1. What various contrasts does Paul draw in this passage?

2. How does verse 6 apply to people in the Christian ministry and those who benefit from their ministry?

3. What are some ways that people imagine they can mock God (v. 7)?

4. Verse 8 is obviously not talking about literal seed. Then what sorts of things are "sown"?

5. What are some examples of both bad and good reaping (v. 8)?

6. Identify some ways that Christians can get tired from doing good (v. 9).

7. Why should "the family of believers" deserve our special attention (v. 10)?

8. How did Paul appraise the motives of the Judaizers who insisted on circumcision (vv. 12-13)?

9. How would outward keeping of the law avoid persecution for the cross (v. 12)?

10. What do you think it means to "boast" in the cross of Christ (v. 14)?

11. What are some examples of "outward" religion that people mistake for true Christianity?

12. How can the church experience peace and mercy (v. 16)?

APPLY

1. In your own experience, what outward signs or works are you tempted to substitute for inner spiritual reality?

2. Consider accomplishments you are tempted to boast about. How can you turn those around and give credit to Christ?

Guidelines for Leaders

My grace is sufficient for you.

2 Corinthians 12:9

If leading a small group is something new for you, don't worry. These sessions are designed to flow naturally and be led easily. You may even find that the studies seem to lead themselves!

This study guide is flexible. You can use it with a variety of groups—students, professionals, coworkers, friends, neighborhood or church groups. Each study takes forty-five to sixty minutes in a group setting.

You don't need to be an expert on the Bible or a trained teacher to lead a small group. These guides are designed to facilitate a group's discussion, not a leader's presentation. Guiding group members to discover together what the Bible has to say and to listen together for God's guidance will help them remember much more than a lecture would.

There are some important facts to know about group dynamics and encouraging discussion. The suggestions that follow should equip you to effectively and enjoyably fulfill your role as leader.

Preparing for the Study

1. Ask God to help you understand and apply the passage in your own life. Unless this happens, you will not be prepared to lead others. Pray too for the various members of the group. Ask God to open your hearts to the message of his Word and motivate you to action.

2. Read the introduction to the entire guide to get an overview of the topics that will be explored. *The Message of Galatians* will give you more detailed information on the text. This can help you deal with answers to tough questions about the text and its context that could come up in discussion.

3. As you begin each study, read and reread the assigned Bible passage to familiarize yourself with it.

4. Carefully work through each question in the study. Spend time in meditation and reflection as you consider how to respond.

5. Write your thoughts and responses. This will help you to express your understanding of the passage clearly.

6. It may help to have a Bible dictionary handy. Use it to look up any unfamiliar words, names, or places.

7. Reflect seriously on how you need to apply the Scripture to your life. Remember that the group members will follow your lead in responding to the studies. They will not go any deeper than you do.

Leading the Study

1. At the beginning of your first time together, explain that these studies are meant to be discussions, not lectures. Encourage the members of the group to participate. However, do not put pressure on those who may be hesitant to speak—especially during the first few sessions.

2. Be sure that everyone in your group has a book. Encourage the group to prepare beforehand for each discussion by reading the introduction to the book and the readings for each section.

3. Begin each study on time. Open with prayer, asking God to help the group to understand and apply the passage.

4. Discuss the "Open" question before the Bible passage is read. The "Open" question introduces the theme of the study and helps group members begin to open up, and can reveal where our thoughts and feelings need to be transformed by Scripture. Reading the passage first could tend to color the honest reactions people might otherwise give—because they are, of course, supposed to think the way the Bible does. Encourage as many members as possible to respond to the "Open" question, and be ready to get the discussion going with your own response.

5. Have a group member read aloud the passage to be studied as indicated in the guide.

6. The study questions are designed to be read aloud just as they are written. You may, however, prefer to express

them in your own words. There may be times when it is appropriate to deviate from the discussion guide. For example, a question may have already been answered. If so, move on to the next question. Or someone may raise an important question not covered in the guide. Take time to discuss it, but try to keep the group from going off on tangents.

7. Avoid answering your own questions. An eager group quickly becomes passive and silent if members think the leader will do most of the talking. If necessary, repeat or rephrase the question until it is clearly understood, or refer to the commentary woven into the guide to clarify the context or meaning.

8. Don't be afraid of silence in response to the discussion questions. People may need time to think about the question before formulating their answers.

9. Don't be content with just one answer. Ask, "What do the rest of you think?" or "Anything else?" until several people have given answers to the question.

10. Try to be affirming whenever possible. Affirm participation. Never reject an answer; if it is clearly off-base, ask, "Which verse led you to that conclusion?" or again, "What do the rest of you think?"

11. Don't expect every answer to be addressed to you, even though this will probably happen at first. As group members become more at ease, they will begin to truly interact with each other. This is one sign of healthy discussion.

12. Don't be afraid of controversy. It can be very stimulating. If you don't resolve an issue completely, don't be frustrated. Explain that the group will move on and God may enlighten all of you in later sessions.

13. Periodically summarize what the group has said about the passage. This helps to draw together the various ideas mentioned and gives continuity to the study. But don't preach.

14. Conclude your time together with prayer, asking for God's help in following through on the applications you've identified.

15. End on time.

Many more suggestions and helps for studying a passage or guiding discussion can be found in *How to Lead a LifeGuide Bible Study* and *The Big Book on Small Groups* (both from InterVarsity Press).

Reading the Bible with John Stott

- *Reading the Sermon on the Mount with John Stott*

- *Reading Romans with John Stott, volume 1*

- *Reading Romans with John Stott, volume 2*

- *Reading Galatians with John Stott*

- *Reading Ephesians with John Stott*

- *Reading Timothy and Titus with John Stott*

Also Available

The Message of Galatians